The Forgotten Survivors

a sister's journey through her brother's mental illness

Dear Wayne,

I hope this book gives you
Comfort & support.

Much love,
Sha Jaccard

SHANNON JACCARD

Published by Shannon Jaccard
Email: shannon@shannonjaccard.com
www.shannonjaccard.com

Edited by Dianne Nelson, Shadow Canyon Graphics
Cover Design and Images by Good Light Creative
Book Design by Tamara Cribley, The Deliberate Page
Book Launch Team Manager Megan R. Fenyoe

The Forgotten Survivors
Copyright © 2019 by Shannon Jaccard

Note: The information presented in this book is for profession, personal, and self-development only. The author is not counseling, acting as a therapist, psychologist, or any mental health professional on the reader's behalf. Reader should consult a licensed mental health professional for diagnosis and solutions. The author is not liable for how readers may choose to use this information.

Jaccard, Shannon, MBA

**The Forgotten Survivors: a sister's journey
through her brother's mental illness**
Printed and bound in the United States of America
First printing April 2019

ISBN 9781796466201

Praise for The Forgotten Survivors

"*Shannon gives voice to an experience shared by forgotten millions. Poignant and raw her words create the space for us to stop holding our breath and say, me too. This book stokes the fire within us to speak louder, lead with vulnerability, and commit to culture change so that millions more do not suffer in silence. As a daughter of a mother with mental illness this book puts into words thoughts and emotions I carry with me every day. If you're carrying such a burden you'll find solace in her words and unity in her experience.*"

Megan Jones Bell, Psy.D.
Chief Science Officer, Headspace

"*Often forgotten in the narrative of mental illness are the siblings of those with serious mental illness. In this thought-provoking, resourceful, and highly personal book, Shannon explains the sibling dynamic within the scope of the entire family by sharing her own experiences growing up with Jeff and those of others she's worked with. The anxiety, anger, and feelings of helplessness often felt by siblings are a part of the unique struggles that brothers and sisters experience. This work is both a valuable resource, as well as a source of comfort, for siblings and all family members as they navigate life with loved ones who have mental illness.*"

David Covington, LPC, MBA
CEO & President, RI International

"Shannon courageously shares her story about the loss of her brother and boldly sheds light into the struggles that siblings who have a brother or sister with a mental illness experience. As a Mental Health Therapist, I highly recommend this book to anyone who has a sibling or a loved one who is struggling with mental health and/or addiction issues."

Megan R. Fenyoe, LCSW
Best Selling Author of *You Are Enough: 5 Steps To Move From Struggle To Strength*, and Host of the *Blonde Bombshell Podcast*

"This book bravely reveals the author's innermost feelings associated with her brother and his experience of mental illness, both the love and the pain. That is what it makes it so relatable to the reader, so compelling, and so evocative. Yet, Shannon puts all that in its place and tells us what was happening behind the veil of strange diagnoses and inhospitable hospitals. More importantly, she tells us what helped her and her family and, perhaps, what could help the reader. It has certainly helped me understand and appreciate the behaviors and the dynamics in my own family."

Bettie Reinhardt, MPH
Former CEO NAMI San Diego
Mental Health Consultant

This book is dedicated to all the siblings who have loved and lost a brother or sister due to mental illness. It is also dedicated to my parents and husband for their support in writing my story and to my guardian angel, my baby brother.

Table of Contents

Introduction

It's wonderful to be a big sister, or as I was often referred to as a 'little mommy.' The day my brother came into this world was one of the best days of my life. When my mother went into labor during the morning hours of August 23rd, I was still asleep and snug in my bed. My father gathered me up into his arms and swaddled me with a blanket. I remembering waking up for brief moments when the cool night air hit my face as he carried me to our neighbor's home. He told me that he was taking my mom to the hospital and I was about to become a big sister. The neighbors I stayed with were like grandparents to me. They loved me, fed me, and my adopted grandfather taught me how to play cards and how to shuffle. It was great fun for any four-year old. A few days later, my parents brought me home and sat me in a rocking chair. They propped up pillows all around my body and placed my baby brother in my arms. It was instant love, and a most precious gift. Even though he was taken too soon from this world, and although his life was a bit of a roller coaster, every moment was a gift that taught me love, strength, and perseverance.

Today, I get the joy of seeing my brother's smile through my daughters.

How to Use This Book

The Forgotten Survivors is not just a memoir but a mix of my story, other sibling stories, and self-help features. The reason I wrote the book this way is because not all sibling relationships are the same. Some readers may be the eldest like me, or the youngest. Some may be twins, or half and step-siblings. Some readers may have experienced love and trauma and some may have lost their sibling.

The first part of the book is the memoir about my brother and me. The second part is short sibling stories with different lived experiences. And the last part explores the sibling experience from loss and grief to advocacy and family.

This book doesn't need to be read from start to finish. You may jump around to the location that has the information and support you need today and comeback for the other areas of the book as you need them.

Here is a breakdown of the chapters to help you navigate.

PART I

Chapters 1-10: Memoir about my brother and me.

PART II

Chapter 11: A compilation of sibling stories from both perspectives of siblings who have a mental illness and those that do not. I added these important stories to my book because not everyone will have had the same relationship I did with my brother. Here you may find another story that speaks more closely to you.

This is not an exhaustive list of the sibling experience with mental illness. A goal of mine is to bring more of these stories to readers. If you would like to share your story, please email me at: shannon@shannonjaccard.com

PART III

Chapter 12: Grief and Loss. For those of you whose brother or sister has passed away, this chapter talks about our type of loss.

Chapters 13-14: Our shared experiences from grief to trauma, spousal relationships, and asking the serious questions like, 'Should I have children?"

Chapters 15-16: I often get asked how to advocate and how to honor my sibling. These chapters talk about the issue of enabling and supporting our siblings.

Chapter 17: Mental illness impacts everyone. This chapter explores how it impacts us (the siblings) and our parents.

All of our journeys and experiences are different. What we are not, is alone. I hope in this book you find some support and connection. My husband described my book the best. "Your book is like a friend talking to another friend over coffee."

In this book, I talk about the good, bad, and ugly, because that is life and that is definitely life with mental illness.

PART I

My Brother

Chapter 1
The Surviving Sister

"A sibling represents a person's
past, present, and future."

~John Corey Whaley

April 11, 2008

The worst night of my life.

My body was limp on the floor, and I didn't think I would ever be able to move again. In fact, I was *certain* I would never be able to move again. I didn't *want* to ever move again. I stared up at my husband with glassy eyes. He had just spoken words that my brain would not register—*could* not register—because what he was saying couldn't possibly be real. I shook my head. I thought I was passing out. It felt like my conscience was just slipping away, hovering above me detached from my body. Is this what people felt like when they were dying? Maybe my husband's words had killed me. But then, no, I wasn't dying. I knew this because, with a slam, my conscience returned as if to make me know for sure this was real. Then I felt the excruciating pain. Being dead could never feel this bad. This was pain beyond comprehension—pain that no one should experience, and pain that no one could even pretend to understand without having experienced it. One night in April, at age twenty-nine, I learned I had suddenly become an only child.

August 23, 1982

I felt that I was floating until the cool night air whispered across my face. I awoke, realizing I was curled up in a blanket in my dad's arms, and he was taking me to our neighbors. "Honey," he said as he smiled down at me gently, "you need to be a good girl for Mr. and Mrs. Thompson. I have to take your mom to the hospital, and we will bring home your baby brother." At four years of age, I wasn't really sure what he meant, but a couple of days later, sure enough, I was introduced to this little bundle with pearl-white, rumpled skin and bright blue eyes. I could see my own reflection each time I looked into them. He was perfect, better than any doll I could ever own, and I immediately decided he must have been brought home just for me. And maybe he was.

I remember the first time I was allowed to hold him. I had wanted to play with him from the moment he came home, so when my mom said I could hold my baby brother, Jeff, I was ecstatic! It was as if she was telling me I was a big girl now, with big girl responsibilities to care for this little thing. My mom sat me in our old rocking chair and put pillow after fluffy pillow on my lap until I couldn't see where I began and the pillows ended. "Okay, Honey, hold out your arms," my mom said as she gently arranged my baby brother on my lap. I felt such pride—such responsibility. In that moment, I knew I was holding something special. This new person was *my* brother. He would be my playmate and my partner in crime as we grew. He would be someone I would always protect, and someone I would love for the rest of my life.

April 11, 2008

Like me, my husband was also immobilized, partly because the news my mother had given him over the telephone hadn't quite sunk in, but also because of me. He sat upright on the couch with his hands in his lap, watching me carefully, cautiously unsure how I was going to react but knowing it wouldn't be anything good.

For several moments, the world as we knew it stood still between us. I was wrapped in my own thoughts, and Greg just kept staring at me. I stared back, but I was in shock. There was no movement between us for what seemed like a long time, but then the remote control I was holding unexpectedly fell out of my hand. I focused on breathing through the swarm of emotions that were filling my body. In and out. Deep breath in through my nose. Slow breath out through my mouth. In and out. Rise and fall.

I have always been a fighter. With Jeff's illness, I wouldn't settle for what the doctors were saying. Instead, I started researching what was going on, started a nonprofit for people dealing with the same issues, and took courses to learn more. I knew that as soon as I stopped shaking, I could fix this. I wanted to fix everything so it could all go back to the way it was supposed to be. I mean, how could any of this be true? It must be a sick joke played by someone with a terrible sense of humor.

I had just seen my brother two days earlier. At the time, he was bloated from all the medicine he had been given. He was sleepy because, as we discovered later, hospital staff had put Jeff in restraints and injected a sedative earlier that same day. We found him lying in his bed completely groggy but at the same time ecstatic that we were there. Although he looked awful to me, I didn't expect him to die. He was in a hospital to heal. Regular people—people like me, my family, my *brother*—we don't go to the hospital to die. We go there to get better. I therefore rationalized that the information I had received was incorrect. I went so far as to believe that maybe it wasn't even my mother who had called. Maybe my husband had thought it was her, or maybe he had misunderstood exactly what had been said.

These thoughts, hopeful thoughts, kept tumbling over and over in my mind, but I knew better. I knew it was true. It had been my mother on the phone, and my husband hadn't misunderstood. I was lying on the floor next to the TV crying and shaking, but I needed to confirm that there was really no mistake, no hope. I decided I should call my mom.

I picked up the phone and dialed slowly and carefully, because I could barely see the numbers through my tears. I felt that if I could just talk to my mother, we would get all of this sorted out, and things would be explained and fixed. The phone rang, and when my mom finally picked up, "Mom?" was all I got out before the tortured screaming was unleashed on the other end of the line. I had never heard anything like this before, and certainly not from my mother. My mom can a bit dramatic at times, but overall she is level-headed and intelligent, and I always felt deeply loved by her. The woman on the other end of the line didn't sound like my mother at all. "He's dead! He's dead! You need to get up here now!" She was screaming, and this was all she could manage to say.

We all wonder how we would behave in a crisis. How we would remain calm and smoothly take control of the plane as it went down, ensuring that other than a few bumps and bruises everyone on board would make it to the ground with nothing more than an exciting story to tell. But this was different. This was *my* crisis—my own surprise and pain. And when you hear the pain of someone else you love—your child, your best friend, your parent—the weight of it becomes immense and unbearable. It is the dense pressure at the bottom of the ocean squeezing and squeezing until the silkiness of water feels like the weight of cement blocks on top of you. It compresses your rib cage, making it impossible to draw a deep breath. It pounds against your mind, making it impossible to reason. So, even though I heard the words, "He's dead," straight from my mother's lips—the same mother who still drives to my house to take care of me when I am sick and who attends my public engagements as a show of her unwavering support of me—I still couldn't believe my brother had died.

To help me make sense of this nonsense, I chose to be the reasonable person in this crisis and decided to call the one person I could think of who could make everything better—my boss Bettie. Everyone looks to Bettie for advice. She always has the right answer or knows what to do. I knew she could make sense of this crisis, and she would know how to handle it.

"Bettie?" I cried out, still confused and hurting but relieved when she answered her cell phone. I can only imagine how I must have sounded to her, yet even by perceiving my own pain and disbelief, she immediately became alert and braced herself for the news I was about to share—whatever it was.

"It's my brother! He was killed at the hospital and I don't know what to do! You need to tell me what to do. I need you to fix this!" My words came out of me in scream-like bursts. In the short, matter-of-fact tone that is Bettie's way, she instructed me, "You need to call the hospital. Ask them what happened. Give the phone to Greg." I obediently handed my husband the phone.

My eyes started to lose focus again and the room began to spin. I tried staring at Greg, thinking that if I really concentrated, Bettie and Greg would exchange some words that would clarify the situation and explain how such a mix-up could happen. Then I recalled Bettie's other instructions—call the hospital. I had a mission. I regained my focus and with intent climbed the stairs to our bedroom to find the phone numbers I used when I called my brother. Jeff had been at the hospital only a short time, so I hadn't memorized them yet. I had to search through a ton of other papers on Greg's computer desk, but I was determined to find the numbers quickly so that I could straighten out this mess and get things back to how they should be.

Once I found the hospital phone number, I frantically dialed and prayed that, once I asked, they would say, "Jeff is in his room sleeping." Then tomorrow I could visit him just like I had planned. The phone was finally answered with a boring, "Hello."

"This is Shannon Jaccard. I want information about my brother, Jeffrey Christopher."

"Hold on a minute," the woman said in a tone that made me think I was interrupting her in the middle of her favorite soap opera. Maybe this was the same woman who had been rude to my mom and me when we had visited my brother two days ago. Or, maybe everyone at that hospital uses the same tone.

April 9, 2008

My parents live in North San Diego County, and it was a pretty long drive for them to visit Jeff. Just two days earlier, my mom picked me up at my house so that we could visit Jeff together. My mom had just celebrated her birthday a few days ago, and we wanted a chance to share it with my brother. He didn't get to celebrate with my mom and the rest of the family because he had been admitted to the psychiatric unit at Sharp Grossmont Hospital in La Mesa, California.

My mom had made a chocolate cake and brought a piece of it for Jeff along with the other usual items—a deck of playing cards, some books for him to read, and a coloring book. There wasn't really anything to do at the hospital unless we supplied it. My brother was a terrific artist and loved to draw, so we always brought something like that for him to do. We also took games along on our visits because it helped encourage conversation in an uncomfortable situation. We knew Jeff didn't want to be there, and we certainly didn't want him to have to be there. But if we visited and just stared at him because we had nothing else to do, he would feel more self-conscious. Playing cards and talking lessened the tension. (I haven't played cards since my brother died.)

We arrived at the hospital and received our visitors' badges. It was a process my mom and I knew well. We walked into the building and approached a woman sitting behind a desk. She asked us why we were there, so my mom explained we were there to visit Jeff. While the woman looked up my brother's information, my mom and I signed in and created name tags. Finally, she let us through to a set of locked doors where we were buzzed in by another staff member.

After explaining yet again that we were visiting Jeff, an older nurse with short, grayish hair and stubby fingers demanded, "Open your purses and let me see what you have." She had no caring or sympathy in her voice. Nothing about her seemed to understand how difficult it was to have a loved one in a locked-down psychiatric facility. I was surprised and disturbed at how callous she was toward my mother and me. My brother had received care from several facilities, and on only one other occasion had we ever been treated poorly. This time was the worst. I felt like I was entering a jail, not a place that was supposed to care for people.

The nurse pointed to a pen inside my mom's purse and said, "You can't bring that in here." It sounded as if she thought she was stating the obvious and that we were either stupid or being sneaky by trying to give a patient something he wasn't allowed to have.

"We need a pen to play the games we brought," my mom retorted in a tone that let the rude nurse know she wasn't going to let her speak that way to us. My mom is a gracious, well-mannered woman, but she is definitely not a pushover, and because the nurse was inconsiderate, my mom decided to give her the same attitude.

"A pen can be used as a weapon. You'll have to use a pencil instead. These people can be dangerous! Trust me. I see it all the time."

I watched the exchange between the nurse and my mother and tried to reason why a pen would be more dangerous than a pencil. It didn't make sense. I shrugged it off, but what really irked me was the immediate, easy statement that the patients were violent. I wanted to argue with this nurse. Her comment was supporting a stigma that people with mental illness want to harm themselves or the people around them, and it was discrimination at its worst. She clearly believed the patients in this hospital were bad, violent people who belonged behind locked doors. She didn't even realize how she was insulting the son of the woman standing next to her.

Because of her ignorant comment, I knew this nurse had no idea what my brother was really like, and I doubted she would care if I tried to tell her. Jeff was gentle and kind. My husband's niece and nephew loved playing with him, and he would let them climb all over him. The two children asked to attend his funeral and acted as altar servers because they loved playing with him so much. My brother had a gift with babies and could comfort them with his touch. Even when Jeff was very sick, he wasn't violent, and it made me angry that this woman could make such an assumption.

My mom gave up arguing with the woman. We knew it wouldn't do any good, and neither of us wanted to lose the valuable and limited time we were given for visitation, so my mom took the pencil and proceeded inside. Finally we were able to enter the last set of locked psychiatric-wing doors, where my brother was being "cared for" on the other side.

I didn't realize it then, but I believe now that the nurse was rude to my mom and me that day because my brother had been restrained earlier that same day. This hospital used restraint as a form of punishment, and I am sure the nurse thought my brother was a troublemaker.

The psych unit was decorated in various shades of gray, and the only deviation was the large, thick glass separating the staff from the patients. The entire place reeked of a lack of caring and of devaluing the human beings they were serving. Interestingly, the doors into the main hospital lead into a room of bright colors, with blown, stained-glass art adorning the ceiling. Unfortunately, the psychiatric hospital is separated from the main hospital, and there is only one way in—the dark, dismal entryway. I do not understand why a psych unit is so drab and depressing. It makes no logical sense. The patients are there for emotional disorders, so why would anyone put these individuals in a place that looks as depressing as some of them feel? I've never understood this, yet there is no push to change it.

A male nurse approached us and said that Jeff was sleeping because he had a rough day. I had no idea what he was talking about, but I could tell that he was trying to encourage us to leave and come back another day.

"We don't care if he is sleeping. We will wake him up," my mother stated in a tone that let the nurse know she had every intention of seeing her son. Now, looking back, I am thankful my mom was confident enough to stand up to that nurse, because that was the last night I'd have with my brother.

When we walked into the room, Jeff was lying asleep on the bed in his boxer shorts. I had to hold back a giggle, because even in light of what the nurse had referred to as Jeff's "rough day," and the indifferent treatment my mom and I had received when we arrived, my brother always loved hanging around the house in his boxers. He was never embarrassed. He didn't care who saw him, and obviously that characteristic had stayed with him no matter where he was.

Mom went over to Jeff and tried to wake him, while I hopped onto the bed, figuring it would get his attention. When he woke, we could tell that he had been given something to sedate him. He managed a wide smile, and it was obvious that he was delighted to see us. Still, the warmth and excitement that I knew he felt did not make it to his eyes. My brother had amazingly blue eyes. They were so blue that people often thought he must be wearing contacts, but at this moment, his eyes weren't that brilliant blue. They seemed dull, and his eyelids were droopy. He struggled a bit to sit up, but with our constant urging and the promise of chocolate cake, he managed to scoot to the edge of the bed. Although he knew it was Mom and me, and he wanted chocolate cake, it was difficult for him to shake the cobwebs that were causing him to move so slowly.

"Come on, Son, put on your robe and we'll go to the other room and play UNO," my mom said, trying to sound cheerful. But I could hear the shakiness in her voice. We both knew something wasn't right with Jeff, but again, being in a psych hospital doesn't promote happiness, so neither of us realized that we should be concerned.

Jeff stumbled a bit as he got off the bed and walked over to get his robe. Mom and I met him at a small table in an open space that was the only area for all the visitors to be with their loved one. Other patients were in the room. They seemed bored with nothing to do, or maybe they were waiting and hoping they would have a visitor, too.

Jeff sat down between us and my mom gave him the piece of chocolate cake. Jeff looked at the cake, and when the nurse on staff passed by, he asked for a carton of milk. As Jeff ate his cake, Mom and I began setting up the game. Jeff looked at me and asked, "Do you want some?"

"Sure," I said.

"Too bad—Mom brought it for me. Just kidding. You can have some, but not too much."

After an hour of playing UNO, which I won, one of the nurses let us know our time with Jeff was up. Jeff hugged Mom and me, and when I told him I loved him, he said he loved me, too. I felt uneasy leaving him there, but I really didn't know what the right thing was, and maybe I was just sensitive from the inhospitable treatment we had received when we arrived. I wanted my brother to get better, and I still believed that is what this hospital would do. My brother would be healed here. Plus, believing my brother was safe here allowed my entire family to breathe a sigh of relief. We knew he was receiving the care he needed.

Of course, now we know the truth. My brother paid the ultimate price in that lesson of lies. We left him in a place that had no warmth, no love, and no hope. Although we were able to eat cake and play games, the hospital had a semblance of "normalcy" only while we were there. Once my mom and I left, it was back to the drab, depressing place it had been before we arrived.

April 11, 2008

After a short hold and a series of clicks, I was transferred to the manager on duty.

"Hello, Ms. Jaccard. I am so sorry about your brother."

Her voice was gentle and sad, and that convinced me, "Oh my god, it is true!" Then it hit me. Even though my husband had told me; even though my mother had told me—it took this person, this manager on duty to make me understand it was real. The weight of those words was like a sledgehammer straight to the chest. I felt I might cave in upon myself, because I knew I couldn't deny the reality any longer. My brother, my only sibling, had been taken from me, from my parents, from the world.

Questions immediately started popping into my head, but as quickly as I thought of them, they were gone. The distress I was feeling was so sharp I couldn't really think about anything other than to remind myself to breathe.

"What happened?" I choked out. I remembered my boss, Bettie, telling me to call the hospital. They would know what happened. I focused on Bettie telling me what I should do, and this kept me calm enough to be able to listen to the voice at the end of the line.

"He had been placed in restraints and was found to be holding his breath and suffocated." Even in that moment, that unbelievable, disoriented moment, I knew it didn't make sense. He held his breath until died? Like some child who threatens his parents that he'll hold his breath until he dies if they don't buy him a pony? I knew that wasn't the answer to my brother's death, but I couldn't deal with truths or lies or facts or fictions right then. I was still reminding myself to breathe.

How could this be happening? Really! I was just at dinner with my husband on a normal Friday evening. Why didn't I know that, while I was at Cozumel's eating a tostada, my brother was dying?

I finally resigned myself to the truth—Jeff really was gone. Because I could no longer pretend it could be anything else, I knew I needed to get to my mom as quickly as possible. I didn't know if she was alone, thinking the same thoughts and feeling the same feelings that I had. I didn't know if my dad was at work or home. Later I learned that my father, who is a driver for FedEx, had learned the devastating news while at work, and he had to make the forty-five-minute drive home to my mother by himself.

Greg grabbed some clothes for both of us, and we quickly left. It was dark outside and the night was cool and clear. The night didn't match the news we had received. Something as bad as my brother's death should be accompanied by a horrific storm, shouldn't it?

My parents live forty minutes from Greg and me in a rural community of North San Diego County. It is where I grew up, and I was familiar with the trip, having made it many times before. I knew Greg was driving as fast as he could, but it seemed like we were not moving at all. From his cell phone, Greg called my closest friends to let them know what had happened. He spoke in hushed tones, and I could hear the voices on the other end react in surprise, but I couldn't tell what was being said. I sat there, looking out the window at the night and for my brother. I urged our car to go faster, but time had stopped for me.

When we reached my parents' house, it looked the same. It was as welcoming as it had always been to me. But it seemed as if there should be something profoundly different about it, because something so profound was occurring to the family that lived in it. It occurred to me that houses were like guards—they protected the outside world from seeing the joys and sorrows taking place on the inside.

My mom was curled up on the couch. A few neighbors and friends surrounded her, and I was relieved to discover she had not been alone. I sat down next to my mom on the edge of the couch, and we cried. We cried together and we cried separately—for Jeff, her son, and Jeff, my brother.

Our family priest, whom we had known for more than fifteen years, was talking and praying with us when my dad walked in, still in his work clothes. I remember Dad standing there as he watched the palpable pain pour from my mother. And I saw the anger and hurt on his face because I knew he wanted to help us, but there was nothing he could do. My dad was strong that night. Maybe his mind was protecting him, keeping him from realizing the truth so that he could be the strength my mom and I needed right then. Of course, like me, he would come to realize that what had happened to Jeff was true, and then he would join my mom and me in our pain. But for that moment, my dad was our strength.

One by one, our neighbors said good-bye and told us to try to get some sleep, but we all knew that genuine sleep would be impossible. I elected to stay away from my old bedroom because it was so near where my brother had slept while we were growing up. I made a bed on the couch. I needed my husband with me, and although it couldn't have been comfortable, he grabbed a few blankets and pillows and placed them on the floor next to me. Sometimes Greg dozed, but mostly we both lay there, hour after hour, private in our own thoughts.

I had planned to visit my brother tomorrow, or maybe it was today. I couldn't remember. My mom had intended to see him Friday night, and I wanted to go during the day on Saturday. I had made plans to see him. It just wasn't possible that he was gone. It took me hours to work through what "gone" really meant. No matter how I tried to define it for myself or mold it into something I could accept, the fact was, "gone" meant I could not touch Jeff, hold him, laugh with him, or speak to him again.

It was too hard for me to think about, so I switched gears to work on the "questions." What had happened? Who was there? Why had he been in restraints? How could he hold his breath until he died? Somebody must have the answers I needed—an explanation of what had occurred. I rolled these thoughts around in my mind. Who should I ask? What steps should I take?

By the time the sun began to rise, I had a plan. I was going to call my doctor for some medicine to help me sleep. I wasn't going to tolerate another night like this one. And when I was able, I was going to call my brother's protection and advocacy advocate. I was sure she would be able to help me find the answers I needed.

April 12, 2008

The next day began and ended with crying. Streams of people came over to my parents' house, each one assigned to watch one of the three of us. I can't write much about this day, because I truthfully don't remember much of it. However, if there is anything I do remember clearly is when my mom asked me to check on my dad. I hesitantly walked upstairs to my parents' bedroom and peeked inside. My dad had been strong for me and my mom last night, but what I saw today was completely different. Dad was tortured. Everything he had repressed the night before had been unleashed. Tears were streaming down his face, and he pounded the bed in what I thought was anger and frustration. I must have made some sort of noise, because he looked in my direction. What I saw and felt was appalling, and I thought there could be no worse suffering than this. It took several moments before Dad realized who I was, but once he did, he began to relax. He tried to smile for me and said he would be downstairs soon.

It dawned on me that not only had I lost my brother, I had lost my parents as I had known them. From that moment forward, I would worry about my mom and dad and their mental and physical ability to survive the loss of my brother. Each time one of them coughed, it would bring a new flurry of fear into my heart. I counted the most important people in my life, and with the loss of Jeff, I was down to three.

Later, through grief counseling, I learned that the loss of Jeff wasn't just the loss of a brother, but the loss of an uncle for my children, the loss of nieces and nephews that I would never have, the loss of my childhood playmate, and the only other person I could complain to about my parents and who would completely understand. The loss of a brother is so much more than just one person.

Chapter 2
Life Before Illness

"Hold my hand big sister all the years
through, Hold my hand little brother for I
will always love and protect you."

~Author Unknown

My brother and I had a typical brother-sister relationship. He would tease me at every opportunity and I gladly reciprocated. For the first years of our lives we lived in Oakland, California, but when I was eleven and he was seven, we moved to San Diego, California. This was a big change for both of us. We had to make new friends and attend a new school, and we were removed from the only family (outside of our parents) we had known. All of my friends in Oakland had loved my brother, mostly because he was so cute with his sandy blond, wavy hair, big blue eyes, and just slightly chubby cheeks. While my Oakland friends and I would gather and play on our own, we never completely dismissed him from our circle, but that all changed in Southern California.

The first friend I made in San Diego was a girl who was an only child. She never quite understood why this little boy was hanging around me, and she quickly found ways to push him aside. I didn't really like it, but I was also eleven years old in a new city, and I wanted to make friends. My friends in Oakland always seemed to love Jeff's company, so it was confusing to me that my new friend was bothered by him being around. However, instead of being upset that a friend of mine wasn't interested in having him tag along, he went out and easily made his own friends. Once Jeff got into the groove of this new Southern California lifestyle, he seemed to flourish. Jeff was like that. He always bounced back—until one day in the middle of his second-grade school year.

My family was in the living room watching television together before we headed off to bed. My brother was lounging on a mattress on the floor twirling his hair between his fingers. This was a habit he had adopted since our move, and we had seen him do it many nights while we watched TV together. It didn't seem like a big deal to me, but one night, my mom yelped, "Jeffrey!" There was shock and concern in her voice, and she was pointing at Jeff's head. I looked at what my mom was pointing at, and there was a bald spot on the back of his head! It was the size of an apple, shiny and completely void of any hair. How in the world had I missed a growing bald spot on the back of my brother's head?

"What?" he replied in his normal, lackadaisical way as he continued to twirl his hair, completely oblivious to the fact that the whole family was staring at him.

"Stop doing that! You are pulling out your hair!" Mom told him.

Jeff looked at my mom in disbelief. I am sure he thought she was joking. He got up from the floor to check out his hair in the bathroom mirror, and when he walked back in, his face hung low. He obviously had no idea that his innocent hair twirling was actually pulling it from his head. He didn't say anything about it, though. He just lay back down on the mattress to watch TV again.

About twenty minutes later, my mom cried out, "Jeff! You are doing it again!"

He looked at my mom sort of puzzled and surprised. He didn't even realize he had started twirling his hair again. He put his hands down by his side, but less than five minutes later he had made up his mind that he would rather have a bald spot than not be able to touch his hair. The impulse was obviously very strong. It was like he knew he should stop, but he'd do it without even realizing it until he discovered a piece of hair in his hand.

We didn't know then, and it wouldn't be until a year later that we'd discover Jeff's compulsive hair twirling had a name. He had developed something called trichotillomania, a compulsive behavior where people pull or twist their hair to relieve anxiety. It usually begins in children younger than seventeen years of age. Most kids grow out of it, but sometimes they don't, and the longer it goes on, the harder it is to break the compulsion. This can cause both embarrassment and depression. Some people with trichotillomania even eat their hair, which can cause bowel blockages. Fortunately, Jeff never did this. There are different types of treatments that can involve behavior therapy and/or medication, or, like in my brother's case, the person just stops doing it. Doctors we spoke to didn't really know what triggered the behavior or what causes a person to just stop.

So, what was going on that caused him so much concern that he needed to pull out his hair for release? He had a loving family, friends, and was active in all manner of sports. He especially excelled in soccer and baseball. In fact, one year he received an award for his fast pitch arm. He loved everything about baseball. The friends, the coach, the sport, and the crowd.

One game he was up for batter. My brother's cute short frame walked up to the home plate and swatted his bat back and forth. His face was set in a determined look. He was going to hit a home run. My dad and my brother used to throw the ball back and forth all the time. Jeff loved the simplicity of the movement and the idea of beating his previous speed. In fact, I stopped playing catch with him because even with the glove on, whenever I would catch one of his pitches my hand would sting afterwards.

He took his bat and hit his shoes shaking off the dirt and dust, just like he saw pros do, and looked back up to the pitcher. This particular day the pitcher wasn't a kid or an adult but a machine. I'm not sure why they made the change. But if I've learned anything in my life it is one decision and one second that makes all the difference. Jeff had his eyes on the mechanical pitcher and braced for the release of the ball. The audience took a collective gulp of breath waiting to see not if Jeff would hit the ball but how far he would hit it. The ball shot out of the machine and hurled its way towards my brother, making contact, not with his bat, but his little face. My mom had to rush my brother to an emergency dentist. The ball had chipped one tooth and shoved another one up into his gums. He came home with a puffy face but also his signature smirk. I thought everything would be fine. He would heal and get back out there again. Jeff never played baseball again.

He lost a sport he loved and subsequently lost the friendships he made with the team. Was that enough for him to start pulling out his hair?

~ ~ ~

He made friends wherever he went, a skill that he had inherited from our mother, and he had a family who loved him. From the outside, he appeared to be a kid who had nothing to worry about.

However, that year was a rough one financially for my parents. We moved during one of California's worst recessions. My parents were each working two jobs to make ends meet, which created stress and tension inside the home. Although my family was very close, and we did many things together, my parents had a lot on their plate to keep our family financially solvent. When we moved, my mother, who holds an MBA, and my dad, who has a BS in economics, were both struggling to find jobs. For the family's sake, they took whatever came along. My mom went into real estate during the day and stocked groceries at a supermarket at night, while my dad worked in insurance and took on odd jobs that came his way. Even though my parents tried to shelter us from the situation, my brother and I could both tell that money had become a problem. A new mortgage and two kids add up.

My brother kept things to himself—he internalized his feelings. Sometimes we would sit at the top of the stairs and listen to my parents argue over money. Usually, I would shuffle him into his room and put him in bed or let him come to my room. One night my dad came home late. I remember hearing fear mixed with anger in my mother's voice. I didn't know what my dad had done for her to be so upset but even at my young age I knew something was wrong. I kept trying to shoo my brother off. He didn't need to hear any of this. Not sure why I felt that I did, but I was the big sister. Actually, I think I needed to hear everything so that I could prepare to fix everything. If I knew what was wrong then I could be the glue to put it back together. That night, Jeff wanted to be protected. I carried him to my bed and placed him in the coveted spot, by the wall.

Whenever Jeff ended up sleeping in my bed, the rule was that I slept by the wall so he didn't roll over and kick me out of the bed. I learned that the hard way with several falls onto the floor! This night I let him lay down next to the wall. It offered him an extra cocoon of being next to the hard, unforgiving wall and his 11-year old sister.

The next day, my mother packed us all up in our questionable brown van and carted us off to church. But it wasn't our church and it wasn't for mass. It was for a meeting.

"You and Jeff will go to the meeting of children who have a parent who is an alcoholic." My mom said. "Your dad is an alcoholic and we all need to learn how to deal with it. Your dad will go to his own meeting and I will be my own."

All this was spoken to me and not Jeff and told in a way that assumed I understood what she meant. I got the gist that this had to do with my dad coming home late and their argument, but beyond that I wasn't sure. Did my dad do something wrong? Is he in trouble? Are we in trouble? Are they going to get a divorce? All my fears started to bubble to the surface but I didn't feel like I could ask my mom and I didn't want to show any fear in front of my brother. Instead, I took his hand in mine and walked inside the room.

There were chairs and tables set in a circle. There was one adult and he started to say the same things my mother had about the group and why we were there. Thought I didn't understand why 'we' were there. I hadn't seen my dad do anything he wasn't supposed to. All I knew was that my mother described him as an alcoholic.

"Let's all introduce ourselves. Please say your name and age and what brought you here today." The instructor looked over at the young girl about my age sitting next to him and nodded, encouraging her to be the first to speak.

"My name is Olivia, I'm twelve years old and my dad is in jail." Her voice quivered and she opened her mouth as if she wants to add more but then quickly shuts down. Her gaze goes to her closed hands resting on her lap.

All of the kids around the room pretty much said the same thing. There dad was a drug user, sometimes nice and sometimes not so nice, most of them had been in jail. But my dad had never been in jail and he had never done drugs. I felt like an outlier or a fake in this sea of pain and suffering. Why was my mom forcing me to be here? The rest of children will catch on that I'm a fraud. My parent's argument last night was nothing compared to the pain of other children here.

"Hi my name is Izzy." Her voice was clear without a hint of fear, shame, or sadness. In fact, as she spoke she sat up more in her chair. I wouldn't describe her as being proud but as if she was resigned to the fact that she was forced to come to the meeting. "My dad is a jerk. He is back in jail after breaking parole. He is addicted to meth. When he isn't on drugs he takes me for ice cream, but when he is, he hurts my mom." Her voice was rote, as if she has told the story many times over, so what is one more time. I never wanted to come back.

~ ~ ~

My brother carried a lot of emotional weight for such a young age. I wouldn't describe him as overly sensitive, but he certainly was more aware of life situations than most boys his age. At times he would refuse certain foods or items if he felt that they cost too much. Although my family didn't go out to eat often, when we did have the opportunity, Jeff wouldn't want to go. He took the burden on himself.

I remembered one day, during the summer, we went out for fish and chips, a family favorite. We were at a shack that was perched on top of hill overlooking the ocean. The sun was shining and you could smell the salt from the beach below. My parents told us that we could each get a drink with our meal. This was a big deal as we were a water only family, and the milk we had at home was de-hydrated and had to be mixed with water. I was excited to get a lemonade that would be a perfect contrast to all the vinegar I was about to dribble on my fish and fries.

"We can't have a drink!" My brother shouted while pressing his palms down on the vinyl table cloth. "I don't want anything. We shouldn't even be here."

"Just eat your food Jeff." I rolled my eyes and looked away from him. This was supposed to be a lovely outing and he was going to ruin it.

"It's fine Jeff." My mom tried to placate him.

"You don't have to get anything," my dad responded.

I got my lemonade with a side of discomfort. Jeff refused to eat, claiming my parents were wasting their money as they continued to fight him on his rationale. All the while, not even the ocean breeze on my face could provide enjoyment in this now tasteless meal.

On the outside, my brother looked like a young boy with a ton of energy. Only now when I look back can I really see that inside, he was struggling with anxiety and poor self-esteem. He feared for my parent's finances, suffered trauma from being hit with a ball, and ultimately was teased for his bald spot by his fellow second-graders.

Maybe pulling at his hair off and on for the remainder of second grade helped him to keep his anxiety under control. For many people with trichotillomania, this can be a lifetime disorder. My brother only exhibited the behavior twice in his life—when we had just moved to San Diego, and once more, very briefly, in high school.

As an eleven-year-old-girl, I didn't know that my brother's hair pulling was related to anxiety or self-esteem issues. What I *did* know was that, when Jeff was worried, he exhibited his stress by pulling his hair. I didn't have any other friends who did this, so

I knew it was unusual. But when Jeff came home from school, he still played outside all the time, loved riding his bike, and he had his own friends. I couldn't really tell if anything was wrong. Jeff sometimes would get wound up over little things that didn't bother me. Though I would get stressed about school work. Just because he didn't get stressed over the same thing, did that make it wrong? Maybe it should have been a red flag. Should I have said something? Done something? Could my brother be alive today if I picked up on some of these issues sooner? I thought he was just unique and I didn't know he might have a problem.

What ifs of the past can send you down a rabbit hole of regret and despair. I know my parents have their own what if's but none of that will bring him back.

As time passed, life moved along like in any normal family. Jeff's stint with trichotillomania ended and his hair all grew back and was as thick as ever. It felt like whatever that was, anxiety/stress, was over. As a family we experienced our ups and downs, our anger and love. The relationship we shared as a family continued to grow and evolve. My brother was entering eighth grade. He was excited about being the big man on campus, even though he remained one of the shortest boys in his class. However, he made up for that with his personality and good looks, and it was a good year for him. In eighth grade, Jeff let his hair grow long, and it had a natural waviness to it. The combination of blue eyes and that hair wreaked havoc on all the girls near him. By the end of the school year, he was voted class clown, a title that would live with him forever. And he knew how to use those beautiful eyes to his advantage. After all, it is hard to say "no" to a boy who can give you perfectly displayed puppy-dog eyes that are the brightest ocean blue. I swear to this day his eyes are what got him out of *so much trouble*. And I know—as all sisters know—how much of a troublemaker a little brother can be.

And then came high school…

Chapter 3
Signs of Trouble

"A moment of patience in a moment of anger saves
you a hundred moments of regret."

~Author Unknown

When Jeff entered high school, nothing unusual happened to him that first year, at least not that I can recall. He began his high school career like all others: taking in new experiences, working through self-esteem issues, and getting used to more difficult homework. I was starting college and was still living at home, so although I was busy, I was around to offer Jeff support if he needed it.

But when Jeff became a sophomore, I moved into an apartment to be closer to the university I was attending. As many siblings know, when a brother or sister moves out of the family home, it is often the first step in dividing the close family life that had been experienced in youth. Changes definitely occurred in the relationship my brother and I shared. I was home infrequently and had a serious boyfriend who would eventually become my husband. However, while distance can create separation in the bonds of friendship, it can't impact the love between siblings. Although my relationship with Jeff was different, the distance didn't stop us from climbing into one of our old beds together on Christmas morning to open the goodies stuffed in our stockings like we had done every year before.

At first, I just heard about regular high school problems, like getting caught ditching a class, not finishing an assignment—typical little issues. As his big sister, I was always a bit worried about my brother, but I just chalked it up to normal teenage behavior. However, by Jeff's junior year, things were not improving, and alcohol was being introduced into an already very shaky situation. He was hanging out with a group of kids who were doing the same things he was doing, and some of their risky behaviors may have encouraged Jeff to go further than he might have gone on his own. And, while I believed the activities of his sophomore year were normal, I also knew they weren't good.

Although I was not living at home, I had an honest relationship with my brother, and he still confided in me. One time he told me that he had gotten so drunk at a friend's house that he had blacked out. He also started to tell me about a rave that he said he hadn't gone to, but that it had sounded "cool." He had a smile on his face that made me suspicious. In fact, I have never been convinced he didn't go to that rave. He asked me what I knew about raves and if I had ever been to one, which immediately made me wonder if he had tried drugs. I was concerned, but I still didn't have any real reason to think that my brother had a serious problem or that he wouldn't grow out of this behavior. After all, when a teenager starts ditching school and his grades drop, or even when a teenager drinks, it doesn't necessarily mean a family should assume it's related to a mental illness.

The first time I really thought something could be seriously wrong with my brother was during a family vacation to Hawaii. We had decided to go to Maui the summer before Jeff's senior year in high school. We were very excited to be there. The weather was perfect, and we loved the location and the hotel pool. I was looking forward to a fun time with my family.

On the third night, we were sitting in the hotel room trying to decide what to have for dinner when Jeff said, "I don't want to go to dinner. I met some guys and we decided to all hang out tonight."

I wasn't surprised that Jeff had made friends, because he had always been a social person, but I didn't understand why he thought it would be okay to leave his family for some newfound friends. Then a part of me remembered his age—seventeen—and that your family was a group you loved, but not a group that was cool enough to hang out with. My parents must have felt the same way and let him go on his own.

After dinner, my parents and I bought ice cream cones and we were lazily walking on a sidewalk that looked out over the hotel grounds and the sea beyond. It was a balmy, fragrant night, and we talked about how perfect it was. I noticed a large group of people eating, dancing, and laughing in an area below us. I pointed and said, "I think that's a wedding reception!"

My parents and I watched the reception for a bit, each of us lost in our own thoughts. Then something caught my eye. "Hey, wait a second! Doesn't that guy have on the same clothes Jeff had on when he left?" I asked.

"Yep, that's his shirt… and his shoes," my dad stated with a grunt, suddenly taking a new interest in the reception. "That *is* Jeff!"

The three of us just stared. Jeff was obviously crashing the party! He was putting food on a plate and trying to sneak it out of the reception site when a security guard caught him. We were too far away from him to yell out his name, so we just stood there a bit shocked at what we were seeing unfold. The security guard escorted him out of the party, and Jeff met up with a group of boys who must have been his new "friends."

Of all the things I taught him—how to ride a bike, tie his shoes, etc.—apparently, I left out how to *not get caught*. Who gets caught crashing a party while their parents watch? Looking back at it today, the incident was pretty funny and one of a kind, but at the time, it led to a sleepless night for my parents. We didn't know where he had gone after being escorted from the party, and he did not come back to the hotel room until 2 a.m. When he did return, he had alcohol on his breath. My parents made a few short, unhappy comments and told him to brush his teeth and get into bed.

My parents honestly did not want me to take on the weight of being concerned about Jeff. They had this perspective until he died, and this was an example of them sheltering me from his behavior. I'm not sure what my parents said to Jeff when they were able to really talk about his being drunk and crashing the party. Now I realize that my parents' protection may not always have been a good thing. While they didn't share their concerns with me, I had known them my whole life and could tell when something was bothering them. As a result, I asked myself a lot of questions and made assumptions. When you aren't told the facts, you make them up. I can only imagine the worry Jeff had caused my parents, but they never overtly showed it to me.

The ability to protect me was something my mom and dad would perfect over the years of ups and downs with Jeff, and this only caused me great frustration. It is an awful feeling to know that, while I was enjoying a wonderful day at with my friends, my parents were at the police station because my brother had been picked up for doing something wrong. I realize that my parents believed they were doing the best thing for me, but it caused me tremendous guilt, knowing that I wasn't there to support either of them or Jeff when they needed it.

By Jeff's senior year, things were even worse. He was getting into trouble a lot more often. He had gotten a few tickets, one of them for not wearing his seat belt of all things. And his friends had completely changed to only those who drank. He didn't participate in any of the typical high school activities, like going to prom, dates, or attending football games. He was still ditching school and continued to drink at parties until he blacked out. He never seemed to understand that his body had a limit to the amount of alcohol it could ingest.

One night, after drinking with a group of his buddies, Jeff woke up with a gash near the lower right side of his face. Apparently, he had fallen down on a gravel driveway as he was doing a stunt while drunk. As he was jumping from the back of someone's car trunk, he made a misstep and fell face-first onto the ground. He didn't even remember what happened, and he only knew because his friends told him. The gash was about an inch in size and bad enough to scar his face for the remainder of his life. Jeff was embarrassed by it, and this might have been the one time when he realized he had gone too far.

Jeff and I were brought up in a "dry" house. Even our mouthwash and vanilla extract were alcohol-free. My dad doesn't drink by choice, but he did as a youth and discovered how bad it could be for him. Although I don't think that my parents worried about my dad drinking, my mom still took precautions to remove any temptation. Later, as an adult, I would drink on occasion, but I never felt the urge to get drunk. Alcohol has always been something that I could take or leave alone. I really didn't understand why my brother loved to drink so much especially when we grew up in the same household. Years later, my parents and I learned that many people with a mental illness use mood-altering substances to self-medicate. I thought that Jeff drank alcohol to fit in, but of course, I had no idea. Looking back, I really can't imagine being a seventeen-year-old young man learning to be an adult while at the same time experiencing symptoms of schizophrenia. Even without an illness, most teenagers don't want to share their feelings with their family. But to have an illness that is highly stigmatized and often misunderstood among adults, you surely don't want any of your high school friends to know what is going on inside. After he was diagnosed, Jeff shared with me how, when he was fifteen, he started feeling that something wasn't "right" about him. Now I realize he was probably scared and maybe ashamed to share some of the internal struggles he was dealing with at the time.

At home, Jeff let himself relax and release the stress that it took him to be "normal" every day at school and in front of his friends. As a result of him trying to control his symptoms in public, my family began to see and experience a more serious side of his illness when he was with us in private. One time, Jeff began to talk about God and being one with the Lord. We grew up in a family who went to church every Sunday. My parents had a large group of friends who got together every Friday to say the rosary before visiting over cookies and other goodies. Jeff and I were both taught to have a relationship with God, to speak with Him, and to listen when He spoke to us. Prayer was a normal and constant part of our lives, and as Jeff started to have problems, I prayed more for him.

My family regularly had conversations about God and religion, so speaking about God wasn't odd. But then, Jeff started saying things like, "I am one with God. God talks through me." He would speak very rapidly as if he had to get it all out before someone tried to stop him. Later, I learned that this manner of speaking is common with individuals struggling with a mental illness. I hated it, and I began to hate God for allowing my brother to become beyond reach. I began to question everything about my belief in God. Was God helping or hurting Jeff? Why would God let something like this happen to a young man? Even at this time, I didn't know the gravity of Jeff's illness or what it would lead to, but I was afraid of the possibilities.

Eventually, Jeff knew that I couldn't take his "God talk" anymore, and he slowly stopped talking about God to me. I forced him to gather the strength it took to be "normal" around me because I couldn't take it. I'm not sure how to forgive myself for that, and I haven't yet, but if you are a sibling or other family member, I'm sure you've had experiences where you just cannot deal with or respond to something your loved one is doing. You feel guilty because of it, but you also have to take care of yourself. This might mean, removing yourself from the situation, telling your sibling how you feel, and seeking support.

Through sheer luck and my parents' perseverance, Jeff graduated from high school. However, as his unknown illness developed and prevented him from reaching his potential, he went from being a B student to barely passing. My parents and I probably suspected that something was happening to Jeff beyond teenage angst, but we hadn't formed any real theories yet. You might ask, "How could you *not* know?" The reason is that mental illness is rarely discussed and definitely not taught in schools, especially not for people my parents' generation. Even though more information is now available about mental illness than ever before, signs and symptoms can still be easily missed. At the time, my parents' biggest concern and focus was that Jeff was dealing with a drinking problem.

Chapter 4
Rollercoaster Begins

"Siblings are the people we practice on, the people who teach us about fairness and cooperation and kindness and caring - quite often the hard way."

~Pamela Dugdale

Life didn't improve for Jeff after high school. In fact, the lack of structure made his life more difficult. My parents actively sought help for him, but because they believed the problem to be drug and alcohol related, they concentrated their efforts in AA, Al-Anon, and other substance-abuse programs.

One Sunday night, Greg and I had just come home from a weekend at Disneyland. It was something we did together every now and then, and when your life is a bit of rollercoaster you need a place to go that can make you smile. At that time in my life, Disneyland was that place. Which is all that mattered.

My mother called when we got in the door to inform me that Jeff was in jail. No amount of Disneyland could soften the blow.

"Since when?" I asked, my heartbeat already accelerating.

"Friday."

"What?" I barely repressed a shout. "And this is the first time you are telling me this!"

"We didn't want to worry you until we knew what was going to happen." Was my mother's break-in record response. This only fueled my frustration more. How could my parents keep something like this from me? I had a right to know as his sister. All this time that I was having a good time, my brother was languishing away in a cell. I felt dirty for having fun. But I couldn't tell her that. No, as the sibling and 'healthy' child, I had to keep it all inside and not let anything out.

"What did he do?" I asked through gritted teeth.

"He walked into a liquor store and stole two bottles of wine and scared the owner in the process." This time my mom's voice trembled.

Even though this situation was beyond upsetting on so many fronts, a part of my brain was laughing. I mean really, wine? He wasn't a 45 year old man picking up wine for dinner. If someone is going to steal alcohol, why would he pick up wine, especially since he didn't drink wine and would have no clue about the monetary value.

"We could have bailed him out on Friday but it would have been $5,000 dollars, and we just don't have that kind of money, and your father and I thought it would be better if he spent some time there to think about he had done." While I couldn't hear my mother crying, I knew she had silent tears going down her face. I could imagine that she and my dad were thinking they had done something wrong. But they hadn't. My parents, Jeff, and I were victims of the system. It is laughable to even say the word 'system' in relation to mental illness. There is no system, there is no community support, there is no legal support, and there is no financial support. When you are left to fend for yourself with no mental health education, the shame due to stigma, and with isolation, the outcomes are bleak.

"I went to the liquor store and talked to the owner and apologized for what Jeff did. He really frightened them. I..just...don't understand it..."

"I know mom, I don't understand it either." And I really didn't. What did she mean 'scare' them? I know he didn't have a weapon. Did he yell at them? Why would he do that. He had never been violent before. The only other time I was aware of him doing anything remotely like theft was in Hawaii when he snuck into the reception to take some food. But I watched the whole thing. He was not aggressive and never even raised his voice. And when the security told him to leave, he walked right out. It felt like I was losing more of him. More of the brother I knew.

"Your father and I talked to him on Friday. He sounded so scared on the phone," continued my mom. "He was begging for us to pick him up." All I could picture was the little boy in my brother stuck in one of the scariest places in the world. Surrounded with people but all alone. I didn't know what the right thing to do was. Did my parents make the right decision by leaving him there? Should they have done everything to have gotten him out? There were no words I could offer up. I was being forced to process all of this after the fact.

"We are going to pick him up tomorrow," she continued.

"I will be there." I responded, leaving no room for argument. I hung up the phone still fuming about the whole situation but without an outlet to vent. I was angry at my parents for withholding information and angry at Jeff for putting us through, yet again, another catastrophe and this time one that would cost my parents money, damage my brother's record, and harm innocent strangers. The spark of hope that he could get his life back on track and heal felt like it was shrinking. And if hope is lost, what would I have left?

~ ~ ~

The next day, my parents and I went to pick up Jeff at the County jail. He was pale, scared, and so grateful to be picked up. He gave me a hug with a cautious smile before sliding into the back seat of my parent's car.

I slid into the back seat next to him and remained silent knowing that he would talk when he was ready.

"I never ever want to go back there, like ever," said Jeff with a shaky and grateful voice as he clicked his seat belt on.

Maybe leaving him there for four days was a good idea. I know that's what we were all thinking and not saying.

"I will never do that again." Jeff must have caught onto the 'we will believe it when we see it' atmosphere in the car because he

added, "no really. I don't ever want to go back there again. I will
N-E-V-E-R do that again!"

"Ok," I said patting his leg. "I'm just glad you are safe."

"Seriously Shannon, I won't do that again." And I believed him.
Did that make me a fool? I always ended up believing in my brother,
but if I didn't, no one else would. They would have labeled him crazy,
thief, non-compliant. And that is how they ended up treating him.
I needed to believe in him for both of our sakes. To allow that sliver
of hope to remain intact, and grow every now and then. However,
Jeff's stealing episode and subsequent arrest was the last straw for
my parents. They decided to send him to a drug and alcohol program in Florida where he would live, work, eat, and pray.

Within a few months of his arrest, my parents had made the
arrangements for Jeff's treatment. By the time he was scheduled
to leave for Florida, his speech was erratic and rapid. He wavered
between being okay with going to treatment and not wanting to
go at all. In the end, he was always the type that trusted his family
and did what they asked of him. My parents were going to escort
Jeff to the treatment center, and I went with them to the airport
to see them off. I took Jeff for a walk, to give my parents some
respite before their departure. Words just flew out of his mouth as
he switched from one topic to another. It was as if he couldn't stop
himself. I couldn't quite follow all of the subjects he talked about,
but one was in reference to God, and how great He was and how
Jeff had this connection to Him. I couldn't understand most of his
rambling. Much later, I learned that this type of talk signaled dete-
riorating mental health. I was scared and confused, but I knew I
had to allow my brother to talk it out if that was what he needed. I
could provide the sounding board, so I mostly just listened. Every
now and then I would try to ease in a word, a thought, or something to bring him back from wherever his mind was taking him.

I was hoping that the treatment center would help him, but I
had my doubts. At this point, I was still uneducated about mental
illness and its signs, but I knew something wasn't right. It was like
Jeff *was* there but *not* there at the same time.

Chapter 5
Is it Reprieve or Is it Guilt?

"If parents are the fixed stars in the child's universe,
the vaguely understood, distant but constant
celestial spheres, siblings are the dazzling,
sometimes scorching comets whizzing nearby."

~Alison Gopnik

"Shannon...hey, Shannon... Shannon...," my brother said with a giggle. Like he had just shared an inside joke that only he understood.

"What Jeff?" I replied with a sigh, letting out the air in my lungs. I was looking anywhere but at my brother. I really didn't want to encourage a conversation. I could tell that whatever was about to come out of his month, was going to be something I wouldn't want to hear.

I was correct.

"Did you know that God, our God and Savior...s-savior.." He stuttered. "Did you know that we are connected. He and I. I and Him." Jeff was now pacing in front of the windows by the airport check-in counter. His arms were becoming animated as he prepared to tell me what he believed to be the truth. That God was calling upon him.

I started to twist my hands together and force myself to not roll my eyes for the hundredth time. This conversation felt like it was on repeat. Each time my brother started to speak about God, I wanted to cringe and retreat. I tried to stare straight ahead and flood out his voice with my own thoughts.

Only ten more minutes and he would board a plane with my parents and be taken over 3,000 miles away. I couldn't wait. That thought was immediately followed by guilt. He wasn't going on a vacation. And I wasn't going to see him again for months. I should have been upset but I wasn't. In fact, I felt lighter for the first time in months. I needed time away from him and his constant conversations about God. Having my brother talk out his delusion about God, did not bring me closer to my religion from my youth. If anything, the pain it brought me created a separation from my belief system. And that belief system had been my support. Not only was my brother falling apart and my parents were at a loss of what to do, but now I didn't even have my faith. Those were dark moments with a sliver of hope that Jeff was about to get the care he needed. However, this hope was also clouded by guilt. Guilt that I was happy he was going to be far away. That my parents might get some sleep. That they would focus on my life for once since his illness came about and took priority.

"Sorry," Jeff said with a clear voice that made me turn away from the window and face him. "I know you don't like when I talk about God. I can stop." He was no longer pacing and looked into my eyes when he spoke.

A part of me wanted to crumble. He was back! A part of me wanted to tell my parents to cancel the plan tickets. He didn't need to go. He was clear now. My heart was racing. Everything was going to fine, right? I didn't know what to do. Should he go so far away from his family? From the people that love him and instead be with a bunch of strangers? But that's what 'the experts' said he needed to do.

"Jeff needs to be away from everything that is familiar to him in order to recover from his addiction." The owner of the Florida Christian-based alcohol and drug recovery farm said. "In order to break the cycle of addiction, Jeff has to be far away from temptation. This time away will help him create new coping strategies."

All of that made sense. If you knew where and whom could sell you drugs then it would be hard to resist. Leaving that world behind for a new one while your body and mind healed made sense. Everything but the separation from his family. That last part is what made me hesitate.

"I love you Shannon," Jeff said and I had to shake my head to refocus on where I was.

"I love you to," I replied. "Be sure to listen to everything they tell you to do. I will come visit you in three months."

"It's time to go," My mom called out to us.

My brother pulled me into his arms for a hug like he always did. I was never a big hugger but my brother refused to leave, even for school, without a hug and an "I love you." He had grown so much since he graduated from high school. My 5'5" height dwarfed against his now 6ft frame. In that moment, while I was hugging my large teddy bear of a brother, I thought back to being the one to carry him around. I would give him piggy back rides, pretend to be a surfboard he could ride at the pool, and horse play with. Now I would be squashed by his size.

"Bye," Jeff said as he walked to my parents and down to the terminal walkway.

I waved and stayed rooted to the spot for a minute before I turned and fled.

~ ~ ~

Twelve weeks later I took the same flight my brother had previously boarded to travel to Florida. An odd combination of anticipation and trepidation floated through me.

Would Jeff be happy to see me?

Would he be angry that I had abandoned him to this place?

Is he healing and going to be able to come home?

Do I want him to come home?

So many questions kept me wired and on edge throughout the flight. My parents were in the seats next to me, but, as usual, I kept my questions and fears to myself. The only person that I confided in was my then-boyfriend but he wasn't with me on this trip.

Technically, I wasn't alone, since my parents were with me, but I was alone since I didn't want to add to their burden. Feeling alone was becoming the norm.

It wasn't that I didn't want my parents to ease my concerns. What kid doesn't want affirmation from their mom or dad. Any sibling that has walked the tightrope between their needs, the needs of their parents, and the ill sibling will understand how I became such a closed box. A behavior that I became an expert in.

Do I ask my parents about this place? Do I ask if Jeff is going to become well again? If I ask, what am I risking? Do I risk my parents health by asking questions that deeply affect them due to their own worries about their son. Or am I risking 'the pause.' The hesitation or pause that lets any kid instantly know that their parents either don't know the answer or are about to lie to them. Either way, I risk having to face the reality that things might not get better. By my thinking, the risks outweigh the benefits and my closed box grew bigger.

We exited the airport and traveled thirty minutes to the place my brother was staying. This place was a non-traditional way of treating addiction disorders. The organization had a network of farmlands, where people with addiction issues could live, work, and heal. The community my brother was at was for men only. The idea was giving both the body and mind a place to heal away from temptation and all things that the person knew. On that piece of farmland, they were insulated, away from anyone that they knew and away from bars and dealers.

We first walked into a conference style room to meet with the administrators of what I started calling, 'the Farm.' The staff believed it was important to also work with families in order to prepare them for when their loved one was ready to come home. That was why we were there. It was family weekend, where we would come visit with Jeff and the staff. Healing was crucial not just for the person but also among the family members.

"Welcome," a man in blue jeans and a polo shirt said. He identified himself as Ray and the man in charge of this facility. "Jeff has had a difficult time adjusting and has kept himself separate from the rest of the men here. And when he does interact, it's a bit stilted and almost combative."

I'm not sure if my parents and I were surprised by his words. I mean, this wasn't the old Jeff, but this was a *new* Jeff we were starting to become familiar and frustrated with.

The elephant in the room that wasn't being spoken but one we all knew to be true, including to Ray, was that my brother didn't just have an addiction disorder, but also a mental illness. In fact, the addiction was secondary to his mental illness. It was like no one wanted to voice their opinion out loud. It was as if we actually said the word, then we were cursing Jeff to live a horrible life without the possibility of finding work, independence, or love.

For my brother, that turned out to be true.

I left blue-jean Ray in search of my brother. I had tired of speaking about Jeff without him in the room. It wasn't that I didn't like Ray but he didn't know my brother. Twelve weeks didn't make him an expert. I also understood that he had to be devoted to the success of all the residents, but I only had to be devoted to one. I found him by himself at the basketball field, bouncing the ball up and down. A mask of frustration on his face after he failed to get the ball in the basket. All my old big sister protections kicked-in. My brother did not take failure well. In fact, he took it as if it was the end of the world. That if he failed once, he would always fail. I constantly worked on changing his mind, and if that failed, then I tried re-directing his thoughts.

I already felt exhausted and I hadn't even said hello yet.

"Hey Jeff," I called out to him before he could throw the ball into the nearby stream. He looked as if punishing the ball would make up for his lack of skill.

Upon hearing my voice, his whole demeanor changed and his face lit up with a smile.

Re-direction it is.

"Hey sis!" He walked over to me and gave me one of his big hugs. In that one blessed moment, everything was perfect. Why do perfect moments have to end?

He had lost weight. I vaguely remembering Ray stating that he wasn't eating and he was doing a lot of praying.

My parents caught up then and said their own welcomes before a bell rang indicating it was time for lunch.

The lunch area was several large ranch style tables that were placed outside on a covered porch the length of one side of the main building. The food was served farm style and everyone, family members and residents, shared.

My brother piled food on his plate and proceeded to stare at it. There was a fight going on inside of him that we were not privy to. In the end, he lost the fight and said he wasn't hungry before getting up and leaving the table. He had not spoken a word or answered any of my mother's million questions.

At this point in our journey, I didn't know what was going on. I didn't know why he was behaving like this. But what I did know is that my brother needed peace.

I silently joined him by the stream. For a while we just stood there.

"Uh..." I hesitated, not sure of myself, as if I was talking to a stranger. But I wasn't talking to a stranger. I was standing next to my brother and it upset me that I would feel so uncomfortable starting a conversation with the same boy that I grew up with. "What do you think about this place?" I managed to squeak out.

"It's good...you know good..." he giggled.

No, not again. I could tell immediately where this conversation was about to go. How could this be. We had a moment. In that moment, he was clear. Why would he allow this stupid illness to control him. Clearly this was all his fault.

The anger was starting to burn in me. And more and more items were being added to that closed box. The box that I locked in a corner of my brain. I was sure it was ok to compartmentalize the box but now it was growing, and I was no longer so sure.

Later I would come to understand that none of this was his fault. That he didn't ask for a mental illness. In fact, I think his salad talk was a release for him. My brother was always more of an extrovert than I. I reenergized. with alone time and he needed and thrived on social companionship. He needed to talk and get out what was on his mind. That didn't mean I had to like it but I couldn't be angry with him for it.

~ ~ ~

I left the 'farm' with the excuse that I needed to get back to the hotel to study. Yeah right, try studying when your brother looks like himself but is a complete stranger. When you know deep down something is wrong but you have no idea how to fix it or if he will ever be the same again. Essentially this was the moment when grief started to kick in.

Grief isn't reserved for the moment someone passes but when something devastating happens that is out of your control and with no potential future of getting better.

I told myself to suck it up. To focus on my work and to get myself back to my brother and try harder. This wasn't about me but about him.

Pep talks to yourself while grieving don't always stick and actually can send you on a spiral of guilt and self-loathing. I went back to the farm the next day and my heart broke a little more.

This time, when I met up with my brother I tried to really be present. Shove my feelings deep down and be the sister he needed me to be. I noticed that his face and personality were more somber, and he was quiet, reserved, and withdrawn. I thought maybe it was because he missed us. The people at the treatment center may accept quiet and reserved as being normal, but I *now* know this was the way Jeff usually hid his illness. However, his speech was calm, and he never mentioned God. He seemed to be on the upswing, and we really believed he was getting better. We all thought that, before you knew it, he would be able to pick up where he had left off. I think this was just the wishful thinking we all go through when we are in crisis with the people we love.

Over the remaining days we took walks, played basketball, and ate together as a group. It was nice to be there with my brother, and the other patients there were very cordial. All of us were working through similar issues, which made the setting very family oriented. And so, we shared our stories. Family members of the men at the facility met and talked through their experiences and emotions, very similar to what happens at Al-Anon.

Still, I had this deep-down feeling that the treatment center was missing something in meeting Jeff's needs. Since then, I've learned that outside appearances in someone with a mental illness can be deceiving. I was blinded by my own hopes for Jeff, and I brushed aside the sad look in his eyes, his hunched shoulders, and other signs typical of depression. Again, I let myself believe that it was because he missed being home and was anticipating the time when my parents and I would have to leave. On our walks, it seemed as if he were looking out into the distance even though he was looking right at me, but even then I didn't think much of it. After all, Jeff was acting as if he was better, and that's what I thought was important.

It wasn't until the last day, when we were getting ready to go home, that my mom overheard my brother saying to another client, "I can't believe they are leaving me here." It crushed her, but my mom thought she was doing what was best for her son.

After returning from the family visit with my brother, my life became hectic. I was working full-time as a marketing director, going to school for my MBA, and planning a wedding. It was a busy time, but life was good. And I knew Jeff was safe. If you have a brother or sister who has dealt with substance abuse or a mental health problem, you know what I mean. Life can be impossibly busy, but at the same time, the simple knowledge that your brother or sister is safe makes everything perfect.

About a month and a half after our visit, my mom called me to say she and Dad were leaving the next day to bring Jeff home from the treatment center. Her voice was calm as she told me this, but I knew something must be wrong. Jeff wasn't supposed to come home yet; we all knew he wasn't ready.

"What? Why?" I asked. Maybe he *was* ready. My heart fluttered. Maybe he had done so well that he was able to come home early.

"The facility director called us. Jeff is exhibiting behaviors that they aren't equipped to handle, and we have to go get him," Mom said, still calm.

My heart fluttered but this time for a completely different reason. Jeff was eating and kneeling and praying so much that his knees had become chapped and bloody. Up to this point, we had only suspected that my brother was suffering from something other than alcohol abuse, but it had been easier to blame the alcohol. Now we had to admit—maybe there was more to it.

When my parents brought Jeff home from Florida, they quickly arranged an appointment with the first of several psychiatrists who would cause us immense frustration. Women constantly wonder why OB/GYNs haven't learned to warm up their hands before an examination, and I will always wonder when psychiatrists lost their humanity. According to Jeff's first doctor, we must just accept Jeff for what he was at that moment, because he would "never get better." He led us to believe that any dream or hope we had of Jeff marrying, having a family, or even having a job was impossible. It was our first encounter with a medical authority in this field, and the idea that we had to learn to live with this challenge because there was no hope at all was mind-boggling. This doctor was giving my brother a life-changing mental health diagnosis with all of its consequences but acted as if he were just reading his temperature. Eventually, we found a much better doctor, but at first, this was an extremely difficult process.

I will never forget the first day I would hear the word "schizophrenia" associated with my brother. I was headed south through San Diego on the 805 on my way to a meeting when my mother called me on my cell phone. Through shaky breaths, she said, "We got the diagnosis today. The doctor says he has schizophrenia." I could tell my mom was in deep emotional pain. She sounded unsure, scared, and out of breath.

I had been doing some research in anticipation of this moment, but I didn't really know what it meant. Most of my research had been done on the Internet or by going to the library. I also had a friend who was studying psychology, and she had provided some guidance. But I hadn't known exactly what I was looking for. I had just studied Jeff's symptoms, hoping to find some sort of answer.

"Mom, it's okay, we will figure it out. Really, it is just a word," I said. In that moment, I think I believed it, but as I learned more, I discovered that sometimes a word is a greater stigma than the disease itself.

Chapter 6

Getting the Diagnosis: What Next?

"Siblings share childhood memories
and grown up dreams"

~Author Unknown

Schizophrenia... we had a diagnosis. Receiving a diagnosis can illicit all kinds of responses—grief, shock, misunderstanding, and horror. Often after the initial diagnosis is given, there is a sense of relief. *Finally* you have a name for what is wrong with your loved one. With this knowledge, you can arm yourself with what is needed to combat and overcome the illness. Right? I'm not sure this applies to the diagnosis of schizophrenia.

Jeff was living at my parents' home when word got out that my brother had this very misunderstood and highly stigmatized illness. All of his high school friends—those with whom he had grown up from the age of seven, ditched him. These were friends who had stayed over at my parents' house and with whom Jeff had gone to high school dances, and who had ditched school with him. These "friends" deserted him as if he had leprosy and would give it to them. They didn't try to understand what he was going through, nor did they ask us, Jeff's family, what to do or how to help. They just ceased to exist in his life. (The SAMHSA website has great tips on how to be a friend to someone with a mental illness.)

Humans are social animals, and while I thrived on reading books and being alone, my brother was energized by being with others. For a person who was voted class clown and who was very outgoing and active, this was probably the biggest blow to his ability to recover from mental illness. Having just one friend remain in contact with him may have turned the tide in his prognosis. He wouldn't have felt so alone trying to navigate what was wrong. He wouldn't have felt judged for not maintaining the expectations of his peer group and for not keeping up with the norms of his age. He would not have felt worthless. At the time, it seemed as though my brother shrugged off the disconnection from his former friends. Looking back, I think he hid his pain well, and generally it occurred with a drink (or two or three) and by smoking marijuana.

Shortly after receiving the diagnosis, Jeff ended up in his first locked psychiatric hospital stay. I will never forget visiting him that first time. I was scared to death, and I wasn't even the one being forced to stay there overnight, away from everything I was familiar with and loved. But, what happened leading up to his forced hospitalization is another memory I wish I could forgot.

I was visiting my parents' home around dinner time. My dad worked evenings as a truck driver for FedEx and my mom was a school teacher. They set up this schedule on purpose so that someone would always be home for my brother's care.

My brother was upstairs in his room while my mom and I were downstairs in the kitchen. All of a sudden we heard a loud thump. Both of our ears perked up for a minute to see if the sound would happen again, but when all was silent we went back to our cooking.

Thud!

Followed by another - thud!

"Jeff!" My mom yelled up to him. "What are you doing?"

Thud was the only response.

We climbed up the stairs to see him jumping from his bed to land on the floor straight onto his knees. For a minute, I couldn't really comprehend what I was seeing. He was purposefully trying to harm his body, more specifically his knees. If he kept at it, he wasn't going to be able to walk.

"Jeff, stop!" My mom and I yelled.

He looked at us with a smile on his face and proceeded to do it again.

"Stop!" I yelled. My voice was full of anguish and I was on the brink of tears.

He looked at me and said, "ok". He turned to go out of his room and down the stairs. Everything seemed to be over but it was like watching an invisible force he was fighting with. A part of him wanted to stop but another part wouldn't let him.

Both my mother and I could see what was going to happen before it did and we tried to hold him back but he was much bigger and stronger.

This incident led to his hospitalization.

~~~

A woman behind the desk checked us in and gave us visitor badges. She pointed the way to the locked unit. Hospitals in general are just not fun places to be. No one wakes up and says, "Hey, I'm going to get a coffee and hang out at the local hospital." In the main building of the hospital, murals and blown glass hung from the ceiling. Warm and welcoming attendants guided visitors to where they needed to go. But the psychiatric ward of the hospital Jeff had been admitted to was nothing like that. Here, the walls were painted a muted grayish blue and the paint was chipped. The only other color was the silver on the door handles. We had to walk down a long hallway until we saw the locked door with a sign and a doorbell. After being buzzed in and walking through, the large hospital doors locked behind us. We stepped into an open room with a sea of individuals in various states of being drugged. Patients were wearing plain hospital gowns and socks. Their movements were slow and sluggish. Many of them had the same far away gaze in their eyes as my brother's. There was one TV in the corner and a few tables. It was visitation hour, and all the patients seemed to know it. When we entered the room, several pairs of eyes looked at us as if hoping we were there for them—that we were people who loved and cared for them. *Many patients never had a visitor.*

When we found my brother that first night, he was so drugged that I could have been dressed as the Easter bunny and he wouldn't have thought anything of it. The next day when I visited, he was a bit more present. We played card games, mostly gin rummy, or we'd go outside and sit on a bench where he could smoke. Most of the staff stayed enclosed inside a small glass room. I'm not sure who was in the fishbowl—the patients at whom the staff was staring at through the safety of their glass room, or the staff members themselves.

Apparently, mental health patients don't deserve the same rights as patient visitors to the rest of the hospital, because once visitation hour was over, you had to leave. My brother tried to keep me hidden in a corner, and I'd stay for as long as I could. But eventually the nurse would find me and ask me to leave. After a hug and saying "I love you," I'd make my exit. The doors closed behind me, making a loud clicking noise. If you've ever visited a loved one in a locked psychiatric hospital, you know the sound I'm talking about it. It is definitely one of my anxiety triggers today. When those doors locked, I wanted to break down and cry, because I was in a state of emotional pain and confusion. Was I doing the right thing by leaving him here? Everyone told me it was, but I wasn't so sure. The pain in the eyes of the other patients made me uncertain if this was a place of healing or a place that would cause more trauma.

After a week, Jeff was ready to be released. The hospital wanted to discharge Jeff back to my parents. My parents and I felt that it was time for him to be somewhere else. *But where else?* This is the second most asked question I get from family members. Where can my loved one live and afford to live? We decided that Jeff would go to a crisis residential home (CRH). Several of these are located in various places in the United States. I am personally a huge proponent of crisis residential homes. Unfortunately, there are too few of them, and they are underutilized. CRHs are places where a person goes voluntarily, and for which they provide a little extra support along with planning for where the person with a mental illness can go to permanently. CRH's are generally a 9 to 10 day stay with a 24 hour provider presence in a home-like setting. My brother agreed to go, and he liked it. It was a large home in a residential neighborhood that was close to the beach. He shared a room with one other person, and mental health staff members were in residence around the clock. But most importantly, Jeff had a sense of satisfaction. He was living and thriving outside of my parents' home. Sadly, it did not last, and I will never forget the frantic phone call I received from the staff.

"Your brother has left! He is AWOL," a therapist screeched into my ear. My first thought was that you cannot be AWOL from a place where you are living voluntarily. Also, I wasn't too thrilled about the sound of retribution in this person's voice.

"Are his shoes still there?" I asked.

"Yes," was the clipped reply.

"Well, no need to worry. He went for a walk and will be back." My brother would leave his shoes to let them know he would be back. I never asked him why he'd leave his shoes rather than something else, like a note, but that was what he did. This is the true power of family. Staff members don't know him like we do. They are seeing him for a brief moment in time. I'm the one who has known him since he was wrapped in a swaddle and placed into my four-year-old arms. I knew his personality, his likes and dislikes, and I understood that if his shoes were there, he'd be back. Like most family members, we knew when our loved ones really needed additional support but were presenting well. Why the medical profession doesn't value the family voice is beyond me. Sure enough, within an hour my brother strolled back into the crisis residential home.

While I believe in the role of CRHs, they are still only as good as the staff, the support they provide to their residents, and the level of stigma that lingers inside any and all mental health facilities. One of the days during Jeff's stay, my parents and I went to visit my brother at the crisis residential home and spent some time talking to one of the providers. The provider's facial expression was very serious, and he seemed ready to impart some horrible news about Jeff's ability to recover. Sure enough, this young psychologist thought it was a good idea to say, "Your son's brain is like a piece of string that has been cut and can never be repaired." When I share this part of our story to audiences, they usually gasp and display shock on their faces. I don't think this psychologist was trying to be mean. I honestly think his training had failed him, plus he was too new in his career to have seen recovery. At this point, I was already a mental health advocate and I had seen recovery first-hand. It is a roller-coaster but a roller-coaster worth living. Still, this well-meaning provider sent my mother into a deep sadness. He single-handedly extinguished the last of her hope.

If you are a mental health provider, I implore you to keep that hope alive for the patient *and their family*. For me, the only time hope is dead is when the person dies. It can be hard to understand this concept in moments of darkness, and it's imperative that the provider community build up that hope both in patients and in family members. If patients and their families don't believe that they can move beyond the dark place they currently reside, then how are they supposed to find the energy and the will to do all the work to make it to a state of recovery? When I think of all the times other people knocked my brother down and each time he overcame it, I feel truly awed and inspired.

Jeff's stay at the crisis residential home lasted two weeks. After that stay, he went to a board and care, a home for people with a mental illness, but a short time later ended up back at my parents' house. And back to square one.

In the meantime, my parents took the NAMI Family-to-Family class. I was driven to help my brother and to better understand what he was going through. It was at this time, I started an organization called Compeer San Diego to provide friendships to persons who have a mental illness. I also enrolled in the local community college to better understand what mental illness is and how to combat it. Jeff was on repeat. We were on repeat.

Chapter 7
Making Choices

"A good sibling relationship is excellent medicine
for dealing with the terrible things in life."

~Dr. Jonathan Caspi.

For all the years I can remember, I have always been a sister. My earliest memories are of being a proud little girl, sitting on our family's green-stitched corduroy rocking chair, surrounded by big fluffy pillows and staring into the bluest eyes of my baby brother. I can still feel my four-year-old chubby cheeks becoming sore from grinning at him while slowly rocking him back and forth.

Having a sibling gives you something you can't share with anyone else—your beginning. You grow up together, sharing your parents' styles, the trials of their marriage, and all the ups and downs of any family. In later life, you share the responsibilities of aging parents and the memories that only the two of you have of family vacations, groundings, and scrutinizing each other's dates.

Growing up, my brother and I played together and got in trouble together. As with all sibling rivalries, there were definitely times when we got on one another's nerves—when he'd copy everything I said or did, or when he'd crawl into bed with me only to constantly move and kick throughout the night (this was the reason I always slept by the wall so I wouldn't fall out of the bed). But our bond was strong enough to overcome our disagreements. So how was it that my only sibling wasn't at my wedding? How could I feel moments of hatred and despair during his last years of life?

How was it that I kicked my brother out of my home to fend for himself on the streets?

No one teaches you how to be a sibling to someone who has a serious chronic mental illness. In fact, when I was growing up, no one taught you anything about mental illness, period. My only knowledge of mental illness came from hearing stories from the movie, *One Flew Over the Cuckoo's Nest*. At the time, my reality of mental illness was derived from stories to elicit fear, not empathy. And certainly, no one talks about what it does to YOU to have a brother or sister with a mental illness.

Life as a sibling doesn't mean you have a built-in friend, or that life will be easier because you automatically have someone to share it with. There is a quote that reads, "The greatest gift your parents can give you is a sibling." For me, there were many moments when I felt that no truer words had been written, but sometimes having a sibling means arguments, hours of worrying, and even times of raw anger. These feelings, as many know, may lead to poor decisions and eventually feelings of guilt. From conversations with many other siblings, these feelings are common when your brother or sister has an illness that pushes them into the center of the family. Even before Jeff was diagnosed with a mental illness, his behaviors and disruptions to the family had already placed his needs at the forefront—or at least that's how I perceived it, and apparently he did too.

Back when Jeff first started to behave in a way that was outside perceived normal teenage angst, my parents had us all get together with our local counselor. In one of the sessions he asked Jeff to organize our family as how he saw it working as a unit. Jeff placed my dad, mom, and myself in a circle, and he laid down in the middle. What he created and how he positioned the family is how each of us felt—and how many other families feel—when one person in the nuclear group has an illness that cannot be easily remedied. When one person is consistently in the center, those on the outside can become resentful. As a result, the one in the center may be overburdened by the constant dictates from the members of the circle. Eventually, many siblings pull away from the circle. They become tired with the rest of the family ignoring *their* needs or with having their input fall on deaf ears. They get angry because their parents seem to be in a constant state of emotional pain and fiscal woes that come with the cost of treatment. Siblings in the circle can feel lost in not being able to "fix" the problem, and they want to return to the way things used to be with their brother or sister. This happens especially to older siblings, and I have experienced it several times. It was like I was at war with myself. On the one hand, I knew that my brother was suffering more than I could imagine, but on the other hand, I was so angry with him, his illness, and the system that I just wanted to run away and start over in a small town in nowhere USA.

One of those moments happened to me on my birthday. We were planning to celebrate at my parents' house until I received a call from my mom. In a strong voice that hid any shakiness she said, "Shannon, you can't come home today. In fact, I want you to stay away until I call you."

"Okay," I said. "But why? What's wrong?" My heart was already beating loudly in my chest with concern. Why would my parents want me to stay away on their daughter's own birthday? There was only one reason—something had happened with Jeff. *Damn him for being in the way of my celebration once again* is what first went through my head.

"Your brother is not well, and we don't think it's safe. I'll talk with you later." That statement confirmed my suspicions, and my mom promptly hung up. I put down the phone, looked at my husband, and started to cry. But this time the tears came from anger. They were like hot beads pouring down my cheeks.

The strong emotions I felt that day have faded little over the years. I was angry, and then, as usual, my anger turned to guilt, and guilt led to worry. Was Jeff going to be okay? Would he harm himself or my parents? Should I do something and ignore my mom's request to stay away? How do you answer questions regarding an illness that no one teaches you about? I wanted to ask God why he was destroying my family. What had my brother done to deserve this type of punishment? I just wanted everything to be *normal*.

Years later, after discussions with other individuals who had similar experiences, I learned that journaling would have been a good coping strategy that day. Instead, I sat and stewed all day long.

Time kept marching forward, and I had never felt so alone. None of my friends had a brother with schizophrenia. Like me, they grew up with the same amount of knowledge on mental illness as I had—zilch. They weren't sure how to help me. As with grief, you never know if you should bring up the elephant in the room or let it lie. They wanted to be supportive but didn't know how, nor did I understand what I needed from them. I learned that I had to dissociate from some friends to survive my own emotional struggles.

When my brother was diagnosed with schizophrenia, I turned to my best friend, who at the time was studying psychology. The first thing she said to me was that individuals with schizophrenia have the highest suicide rate. Those are far from the comforting words I was seeking. Other friends of mine who had known my brother while growing up all of a sudden became hesitant to be around him. On the other hand, I was blessed to have a handful of good friends who were there for both me and my brother. They would come with me to the hospital visitations when he was stuck on the inside. They were the ones who played games with him, laughed with him, and never treated him like a pariah. These are my true friends who helped me survive.

But being alone for the most part, and uneducated on mental illness, led me to make decisions that may have turned out differently if I had just one other friend who had walked in *my* shoes before.

One of those decisions happened in the weeks leading up to my wedding. I always imagined that my brother would be standing up at the side of the altar, beside my soon-to-be husband, in a suit and tie, smiling at me while I approached with our dad. I imagined that he would make a toast at the reception and make all the guests laugh with his wit and humor, telling stories about what the two of us shared in our youth. I could see him dancing with all the ladies, not shy at all that he didn't really know the footwork. These simple dreams were crushed and instead, my brother was an empty seat at the head of the table. His smile was missing from the family wedding pictures. He missed the scene where my husband smashed cake in my face. He never even saw the dress. Greg and I were married for five years before my brother was killed, but his absence on that day was like a little death.

So why wasn't he there? Jeff's diagnosis had been made two years earlier. My family and I were still in a state of shock, reeling from the diagnosis and not knowing what to do or whom to trust. At some point, you have to trust someone, and why not the men and women with doctoral degrees behind their names? At the time of my wedding, Jeff was in a locked-down hospital. He wasn't doing badly, but his psychiatrist and psychologist both advised us that the wedding would be too much for him. And, I wanted one day that was about me. Some girls grow up dreaming about the perfect wedding with flowers and decorations. I wasn't that girl. But I *was* the bride. Was it too much to ask that, for this one day, I receive my family's undivided attention? A day that Jeff's illness could not taint in any way? I wanted to believe that the doctors were right in keeping him away from us that day.

I was both right and wrong. The day was perfect. I woke up to a beautiful, sunny sky. My mom came over early to help me with the dress and makeup. The church was gorgeous, and everything seemed perfect. We danced at the reception until they kicked us out. Of course, there were a few heavy drinkers and some interesting dancers, but no one was talking about schizophrenia, mental illness, or my brother. My parents were there for me completely. I didn't sense a moment when they were concerned about Jeff's well-being. I wanted that one day for all of us, and I got it.

Every day afterwards, though, when I think about that perfect day or look at the beautiful pictures, I remember that I agreed—I made the final decision that Jeff should not be there. I remember that the weeks after the wedding, when he was once again out of the hospital, he said to me, "How messed up is it that they kept me from my only sister's wedding." And, once again, I cried. I'm still not sure if keeping Jeff away from my wedding was the right decision or not; but there are no take backs or do overs. My wedding was a once-in-a-lifetime event. My one friend said to me that we'd have an after-party that Jeff could attend, but that never happened and now it's too late.

Navigating the unknown waters of mental illness is like swimming in the ocean during high tide. Wave after wave keeps beating you down. You have the time to take a single breath before you are pushed underneath the current once more, hoping that your strength will not wane until you make it to the soft, sandy shore.

I wish I could say that my decision about my wedding was the only one that I look back on with doubt and mixed emotions, but there were several others. The one that remains in my mind the most was the night I kicked out my brother from my town house. At this point, my husband and I had been married for a few months. Jeff was once again at another new facility where the primary focus was drug and alcohol abuse. He didn't want to be there, and I'm not sure the staff really wanted him there either. So he left and made his way to my parents' house. My parents refused to let him stay and wanted him to return to the facility. Instead, Jeff came to my place. My mother called me to let me know what was going on and to warn me that Jeff might show up at my front door. She and my dad directed me to not let him stay the night— that he needed to make the decision to take charge of his own life. In a way, it was like that old philosophy of needing to let the person you love hit rock bottom in order for him or her to find the way back to the top.

Sure enough, several hours later I heard a knock at the door. My brother strolled in the front door like he didn't have a care in the world. I think he was genuinely happy to be there. I let him in but promptly told him that he wasn't allowed to stay the night. And for some reason that didn't dampen his mood. He seemed to accept it as normal.

"Let's find you a shelter for the night," I suggested.

"Okay," he replied with a shrug. He was willing to try and find a place but didn't seem to care whether or not anyone would take him in.

"I'll dial the numbers, but you need to talk to them," I said. I called our local access and crisis line that was supposed to answer mental health related calls. I put the phone on speaker so I could help him if necessary.

"My name is Jeff. I have schizophrenia, and I'm looking for a place to sleep tonight," he told the woman who answered the phone.

"First, I need to gather some information," came the reply. She went on to ask Jeff questions, which he answered. He then repeated his request for lodging.

"You can only go to a shelter if you have a mental illness and are homeless," she stated, her voice full of disbelief.

"I have schizophrenia and I am homeless," he replied.

Her response was, "You don't sound like you are." I was floored in disbelief. She was making a judgment call about the level of need based on my brother's voice! Needless to say, she was no help, and I reported the call to the director of the help line the next day.

We called several other temporary housing shelters, but none of them had space. Jeff was told to be there by 6 am in the morning. To this day, I still don't understand this 6 am "rule." So if you need a place for the night, you must be there in the morning the following day?

I was at a loss. Should I let my brother sleep in the extra bedroom or fulfill my parents' request that he make his own way? In the end, he left and I cried. He wasn't even mad at me. He knew this was the will of our parents and made his peace with it. I was the one in turmoil. The only saving grace was that he showed up the next day bright and early and ready for breakfast.

Again I wonder—if I wasn't so alone or knew that millions of other siblings were going through the same ups and downs that I was experiencing, could they have helped me chosen a different path?

When you have a brother or sister with a serious illness, some of the dreams you have for the future start to die even in life. I wanted to have kids, and I wanted Jeff to have kids. They would all play together. I wanted to be the aunt who spoiled my nieces and nephews. But, as Jeff's illness progressed, so did the loss of hope that these dreams would become realities. I wish someone had told me that I was experiencing a form a grief. When I was in these moments of pain and suffering, I *was* in fact grieving. But no one tells siblings anything. We are left to paddle through our emotions with little to no support from family, friends, co-workers, or neighbors. Unfortunately, this lack of support has led to many siblings separating themselves from their families. If you need to take time away, do it. Your pain is real, and you need to take care of yourself as well. *But then come back.* You don't want to be apart for the next twenty years because of your resentment, hatred, or pain you felt for your brother or sister due to an illness he or she didn't ask for. You may turn around one day and realize that you've missed all of this time together—lost Christmases, birthdays, and other celebrations.

One day, I was working a booth for NAMI San Diego at a health fair. A woman, like many others, was walking by the booth, kind of looking at the information but not really wanting to approach me or make eye contact. Eventually she meandered over and we began to talk. I told her about my brother and why I became involved with NAMI. Before I knew it, this fifty-something-year-old woman was crumbling in my arms, sobbing unstoppable tears, like she had never been able to release them before. She told me that she had a sister with schizophrenia and had recently been thinking about her. She hadn't talked to her sister in thirty years. She decided that she wanted to reunite with her sister, and I hope she did. However, she can never bring back those thirty years. This is what I've learned that unresolved anger and lack of support can do to siblings. They separate us from those we love the most, even if a part of us is longing to be with them.

I needed the support, and so do you, because I went from being a pair to an only child six years before my brother's death.

Chapter 8
In the meantime...

Siblings are built in friends. Mental illness can feel like a lake that separates us. Build a raft.

For several months, everything was going okay, and then one day my brother took the bus to the beach. He actually became very good at navigating the bus routes and could make it from my parents' house to mine. It took him three hours by bus for a forty-five-minute car ride, but he did it—oftentimes, unexpectedly. My brother was a people person, so he enjoyed riding the bus and going to the beach. I would even say he was an extrovert despite his illness. You could always find people at the beach. The long stretch of sand, the shops on the pier, and water's waves entice many people to partake. Since my brother lacked a group of consistent friends, this was a place he would seek out others.

This desire for friendship landed him in trouble sometimes. He was at the beach because there were people there who didn't know him or his label. But they weren't interested in being his friend either. So he stayed into the night and then walked to the end of the pier and jumped into the water. This didn't end well for anyone. Fortunately, Jeff was fine, but he scared the people around him and they called the police. The police weren't happy that he had jumped off the end of the pier, because he could have been seriously hurt. I don't think he was trying to hurt himself. He simply wanted to have fun and get some attention. Maybe things would have been different if he had lived into the digital age, but he died before everyone was equipped with an iPhone. Would online friends have made a difference? Would he have felt connected to someone? Anyone?

After my brother's little stunt of jumping off the pier (which, I have to say, I am still stunned he did it), he ended up in another locked hospital ward. This led to a longer stay at a long-term treatment facility. This one was a step up from the look and feel of a jail, but it was still locked and almost everyone there was on some form of conservatorship.

Conservatorship is essentially taking a person who is over the age of eighteen and stripping him or her of all their rights. In the eyes of the law, these individuals are now under the age of eighteen. They can no longer make any decisions on their own behalf, including whether or not to take medicine, where to live, and if they want to drive and/or vote. There are two ways to be placed on conservatorship—public or private.

At this point in time, my brother was the only person in the facility who wasn't on conservatorship; however, all of his care providers thought this was the best place for him to be. At this long-term treatment facility, they had a "step down" procedure. If you abided by their rules, then you earned privileges. *Please read that sentence again.* I'm talking about grown-ups who are suffering due to a mental illness being treated no better than kindergartners when it comes to their rights. And it's no wonder individuals don't seek out treatment when they need it.

Just like with locked inpatient hospitalization, these facilities allowed for family visitation. On August 23, it was my brother's twenty-first birthday. Most of us remember our twenty-first birthday (or don't remember due to inebriation), but I bet you didn't spend it in a locked facility. Well, Jeff didn't want to either. During the day, my parents, my husband, and I went to the facility and brought a chocolate cake with us. After we checked in and had been admitted to the common area, a middle-aged woman approached my mother and started to talk to her as if they were long-lost friends. My mother handled the situation very well considering the woman was naked. We soon learned that many of the patients at this facility ended up in a state of undress, including my brother. I'm not sure why this was the case, but my guess is that it was something that the patients could control. When so much had been taken away from them, whether to be dressed or not was an actual decision they could make.

We ate the chocolate cake outside, and Jeff was allowed to open two gifts. He gave us appreciative smiles that weren't quite in sync with his eyes. He clearly didn't want to be there on his birthday. I didn't blame him. My brother's room had a window that was also locked. Somehow, that night, my brother broke out of the window in his room. He walked down to the bus station, and a couple (who will never fully understand how much their two dollars meant to our family) gave him enough for a bus ride to my parents' house. He showed up there late at night and spent the night, and in the morning he was ready to return to the long-term treatment facility.

About two weeks later, Jeff was still at the facility, and the staff would end up being very grateful for his presence. San Diego is known for wild fires due to years of drought and being directed by water authority to conserve water. No one had been watering their yards for years. A wild fire was sweeping throughout the county and was hitting rural areas hard. The facility where my brother lived housed 100 patients, and they were all in the path of the fire. They waited until the flames were nearly upon them before evacuating the facility. We couldn't even get to Jeff because the fire blocked the roadways and was about to jump the freeway. The residents and staff evacuated to a nearby high school, and Jeff was an important part of the evacuation process. This was where my brother was really himself—when other people were in need. Other patients were scared and feeling vulnerable. Jeff had a way of putting people at ease. He was given a task and made to feel valuable, and he showed them how valuable he really was! People put expectations on him, and he lived up to them.

I wish I could end this chapter by saying how my brother overcame each and every one of his trials—that this hardship just made him a stronger, better person. In some ways, it did. He kept trying different jobs, only to lose them again. He started making friends with homeless people, because they accepted him without reservation. And he also maintained his faith, which admittedly is better than I've been able to do since his passing. But you can only kick a person so many times until they don't have the strength to get back up. I noticed my brother was beginning to mentally distance himself more from reality. Maybe it was his way of protecting himself.

Still, my brother, your brother—they are stronger than we know. Jeff saw and experienced much more than I will ever understand, and he continued to persevere. His strength gave me strength that I turned into advocacy.

Chapter 9
Help and Healing?

"When you can't look on the bright
side, I will sit with you in the dark."

~Author Unknown

Six months later, Jeff did another two-week stint in the joint. (Let's
be real here-- psychiatric hospitals look and feel like jails.) He was
then discharged back to my parents. You can imagine after your
loved one's first inpatient hospitalization, you would feel hopeful.
Your thoughts might run like: "They wouldn't have discharged him
if he wasn't all better, right?" "Now that he's all better, he can go
back to school or work." For us, this was partly true. We had more
knowledge about the illness, and Jeff had been placed on medicine
that seemed to be helping him think clearly. For my parents, this
meant that it was time for Jeff to pick up his life where he had left
off. He needed to work or go back to school. Their efforts turned
out to be colossal failures.

Like many families, we just didn't know what to do. It seemed
sensible to us to get this nineteen-year-old back on track and meet
society's expectations for being a productive adult. At some point,
I think it *would* have been beneficial to my brother's overall health
to work or receive education. In fact, research has shown that the
number-one tool of maintaining recovery from a mental illness is
having employment. Looking back to that moment, Jeff needed
time—time to figure out this new brain he was having to navigate
on a daily basis, time to accustom himself to being labeled with

an illness that caused such a dramatic dissociation from his peers. And time to just *be*. It is often said that sleep is the best medicine for physical health conditions. While we don't know what causes mental illnesses, we do know that the brain is an important and wondrous bodily organ. Maybe Jeff needed to be left alone to sleep, eat, and not have any responsibilities for awhile. In fact, the original state psychiatric hospitals were set up as a place of refugee from all the stresses in life.

Jeff was encouraged to enroll in a community college. My mom helped him sign up for classes, and he was put in touch with the department that assists students with special needs. While I have seen some improvement in supporting students with mental health issues in college, in general, these individuals have to fend for themselves. To add to the dilemma, the term "special needs" tends to refer only to physical ailments and handicaps. Jeff couldn't focus in class and was often disruptive. He wasn't able to complete the homework, and ultimately he dropped out of school.

It became apparent that school was not in the cards for him, at least not yet. My parents told him that he had to get a job. Jeff was medicating *himself* with drugs and alcohol, and my parents took the common route that has been taught to parents for ages when dealing with an adult child who has an addiction. They gave an ultimatum—get a job or get out. And thus began our never-ending cycle: partial wellness, get a job, increase drug usage, get fired from job, de-escalation of mental health, hospitalization, repeat. Does this sound familiar?

Jeff complied with my parents' wishes and got a job doing custodial work at a fast food restaurant. He only lasted a month before being terminated and his mental health started a downward spiral. I'm not saying that the job and subsequent firing are the only factors that caused him to decompensate. There are many reasons, including stopping his medication, having drug interactions, and dealing with a lack of social support. His mistreatment by the rest of the working staff partly contributed to his mental unwellness. He was constantly bullied and harassed by his co-workers for being "slow."

They made fun of him because they needed to instruct him on how to sweep, a task that, in their opinion, should be a no-brainer. My brother saw a job as a place to replenish his diminished pool of friends, but what he experienced instead were hateful comments like being called "stupid" or "dumb." He was ostracized from the other co-workers. While he presented these situations to me like it was no big deal, I know that it impacted his self-esteem and self-worth, which had already taken big hits.

Things didn't improve over time. At the beginning of the Christmas season, dark days came knocking on our door. Jeff would make a beautiful arrangement of food and then decide he was not worthy of eating it. He would then walk up to his bedroom and pray. He spent hours genuflecting on his knees, which caused severe damage to his skin and joints. The moments when he would jump from his bed and land on his knees were the absolute worst. The damage he continued to do to his knees and an impromptu visit to Mexico led to another inpatient hospitalization.

This time, we were no longer newbies to the ins and outs of hospital protocol. Also, I had become much more active in the local mental health community. I admit that a part of me was angry with Jeff. Why was he damaging his body? Why was he putting us through this? Didn't he love me enough to get better? I felt like I was being forced to sacrifice my time, resources, and health for him when he could just make it all stop. But as usual, I would keep my feelings bottled up and trudge along.

Jeff's hospitalization started out like any of the previous ones. Meds for him, nightly visits for me. However, this time Jeff's doctor recommended that we place him on conservatorship. *Conservatorship* is a form of legal guardianship, appointed by a judge to manage the financial affairs and/or daily life of another due to physical or mental limitations. My mother was very hesitant but everything that I had read on it made it sound like a good idea. I mean someone else would help guide Jeff in his mental health care! It could give my parents the reprieve they needed. I thought I knew what I was recommending and that it would be the right decision. In order for Jeff to be placed on conservatorship, a judge had to agree. I kept telling Jeff to just say yes, when the judge asked if he was ok with being placed on conservatorship.

I will never forget the day of the court hearing. Jeff was still in a locked facility and had to be brought into the courthouse. My dad and I were waiting at the court house to meet him there. I expected that he would walk in with a member of the hospital staff. What happened shocked me.

The elevator door rang and a gurney with a man strapped to it came through the doors. At first I was confused. Why was there a gurney at the courthouse? And then I realized the man in the gurney was my brother and everyone was watching him.

He was wearing a smile on his face but it was so upsetting to see how at ease everyone was with humiliating my brother in front of so many people and there was nothing I could do.

Eventually his name was called before the judge. The hospital staff removed the straps from the gurney and let Jeff walk inside. The judge asked Jeff if he was willing to be placed on conservatorship and for a moment my dad and I were holding our breaths while we waited for his response. We let out our breath after he responded affirmatively. Jeff trusted me with this decision and know I was second guessing myself. But when it comes to mental illness sometimes you don't have time to process one crisis before the next one begins. After the court hearing the hospital staff took Jeff away and we left the courthouse with our rights as family members removed.

~ ~ ~

It was the Christmas season and the ward was fairly empty, with just a handful of other patients. People often believe that winter and the holidays can bring on mental health issues, but in general, people are able to work through this time only to deplete their energy later in the spring. Mental health hospitals in the spring months tend to be the busiest.

It was Christmas Eve. My brother's doctor was very aware that, for him, family was important. In fact, Jeff wrote "family visits" as a PRN (stands for "pro re nata," Latin for "as needed") on his medication list. Since the hospital was only a third full, the doctor was able to work out a family visit at an earlier and longer time than the hospitals usual one hour evening visitation. My mother showed up first, was given her visitor badge, and was buzzed in. My husband and I showed up about fifteen minutes later. We both checked in and received our visitor badges before being buzzed in. We immediately saw where my mom and brother were sitting at one of the three tables in the general open area. As we sat down, a nurse started running toward us, yelling that we couldn't all be there—that Jeff was only allowed two visitors at a time. I sat down in a state of shock. First, the facility is a locked ward. We didn't let ourselves in, which means that the staff did and therefore knew the number of visitors. Second, this had been arranged *by my brother's doctor*. And third, it was Christmas Eve. My brother was tucked in a locked facility over a major holiday, and we were visiting him. The nurse was going to head home that night and be with her family on Christmas morning; Jeff was not. Her complete lack of compassion was disturbing, but at this point it was not surprising. My mom called my brother's doctor, and everything was straightened out. The issue now was that this nurse needed to save face and therefore continued to be difficult during our visit. What this nurse wasn't aware of was who I had become in the mental health community. I contacted the leaders of this hospital to report the lack of empathy my family and I experienced at their psychiatric unit. I admit, it felt really good to be a mental health advocate!

During my brother's lifetime, he was a patient in most of the psychiatric hospitals in our area. But if I wrote about each experience, you might get bored, since they were all pretty much the same. The predominant belief of the staff members I engaged with at the psych hospitals was that the patients would never recover. One staff member said to her friend in front of my brother, myself, and several other patients and family members, "I got get out of here before I turn as crazy as all of them."

There was also a lack of support for what the visiting family was going through. This along with a general depressive atmosphere that made you feel as if you were suffocating until you had walked out through the large metal doors. Once you heard the loud clicking noise indicating that the doors had locked behind you, you knew without a doubt that, once again, you had just left behind a very loved person. I'm proud to say I've seen improvement in some area hospitals, but there is a long way to go in separating out a place of healing from a place of punishment.

Chapter 10
Dark Side of Stigma

Christmas was over and Jeff was still in the hospital, but this time he was on county conservatorship. I believed, with my limited understanding, that he would get better under conservatorship. I mean, how could it hurt to have more people help him? People who were more educated about mental illness than we were. Little did I realize that Jeff wasn't going to walk out of that hospital. This time, when he was at his most vulnerable, he would die in a place that we trusted to take care of him.

In the four months before his death and hospitalization, Jeff decided to go to Mexico by himself. I'm not sure why he choose to go there, but probably because he was bored, didn't have any friends, and wanted something to do. We were very lucky because the authorities in Mexico realized he was not mentally well and sent him back to the US where he was hospitalized at a county facility. The staff looked up his previous record and they were able to move him to another hospital that we were all more familiar with. For all his cycles of hospitalization this seemed to be a good start to what could have been a much worse situation. I remember feeling hopeful that so many pieces had fallen into place.

When I first visited him at the hospital I wanted to chew him out for going to another country by himself and with no identification, but as usual, the first few days he was heavily medicated and my anger toward him deflated. He couldn't even concentrate enough to play our favorite card game of gin rummy. I remember looking at this face, trying to find signs of life within my brother. He would just sit there and stare past me, not bothering to wipe the small drops of drool running down his chin. All I could do was be there with him by his side.

After Christmas and the conservatorship hearing at the court-house, Jeff was moved to another ward, and started making some new friends. It was a part of the hospital where younger patients stayed. The whole setup was geared towards youth and my brother's personality started to shine through. He was always an extrovert so to be able to make friends was crucial to his mental health recovery. I remember feeling that if I missed the visitation hour for the evening it would be ok because he had someone else to talk to. It felt like I was releasing a breath that I didn't realize I was holding in. It was a mixture of progress and hope. For the first time in a long while my tension eased I was able to get real deep sleep.

But hospitals are not set up for long term psychiatric care. Their goal is to stabilize the patient and move them to treatment outside the hospital. And two months later Jeff was still there. The hospital decided that Jeff's current doctor wasn't pushing him hard enough to progress and removed him from Jeff's care. We as a family fought back, but since Jeff was on County conservatorship, our rights had been removed. The conservator's office approved the change in doctors against our judgement. This was my first indication that things were not going to be ok. Why would they remove a psychiatrist that Jeff had a relationship with for a total stranger? A stranger that didn't know his family or his history.

His new younger doctor added a cocktail of medicines to his regime and moved him to a different hospital saying that Jeff was getting too comfortable at the other one. In fact, one of the nurses at the other hospital used to buy him skittles at night from the vending machine. My brother loved candy! It was such a minor thing, but I will be forever grateful for the kindness this nurse showed my brother. The doctor, however, wanted to motivate Jeff to live and function on the outside. I could understand the motivation part, but I didn't understand the need to push him out the door. Was it in Jeff's best interest to be discharged or staying at the hospitals?

The new hospital divided their psychiatric hospital into two parts. Jeff was housed in a much smaller gray-walled wing of the psychiatric ward. There was nothing warm and comforting here. And yet, if you walked into the main hospital for physical health care, you would find the ceiling was like that of the Bellagio in Las Vegas covered with beautiful blown glass artwork.

When my mother and I visited Jeff, the women checking us in went through our purses and took out my pen. She condescendingly held the pen in front of me and said, "You don't know how dangerous these people can be." I'm not sure who she thought she was talking to. Did she realize she was telling a mom and sister that either their son/brother was a danger or that he was IN danger?

Jeff was at this hospital for less than a week. On the night of his death, Jeff had been visiting with my mom. Her birthday had been a few days prior and she brought him some chocolate cake so that they could celebrate together. That night, I decided to let my mom visit with my brother alone and I planned to visit him the next day. When my mom was there, Jeff began to get agitated and wanted to go on a smoking break. The staff told him he had to wait a few more minutes and instead gave him an Ativan. Ativan is a commonly used and strong anti-anxiety drug. Jeff was still upset about the smoke break, so the staff asked my mother to leave in order to 'work' with him.

She said a quick goodbye and walked out to the parking lot. Unbeknownst to her, as she sat in the parking lot crying, they put my brother in a 5-point face-down restraint and followed up the first drug with another shot of medicine. They left him alone, in a grey, four walled room tied down to a bed. The last thing he saw before he died was a bare wall. He died alone in that hospital without the comfort and support of anyone around him.

It wasn't even until after his death that I learned about restraints and their usage in psychiatric hospitals. I had no idea that my brother had been placed in restraints before. He never spoke of them. Of all the "what ifs" that have plagued me since his passing, this one keeps popping back up. What if he had told me they were doing this to him. Would I have spoken up? And more importantly, why did he never share it with me.

Each time I would visit my brother I would ask the nurse how he was doing that day. Some days they said he was having a bad day. It was only after I received all the hospital records from his prior stays, and read the notes that indicated he had been restrained previously, did I piece together that 'bad day's' equated to restraints.

The medical analysis would later rule his death a heart attack. The report went on to explain that he had a cocktail of drugs in his system that they administered into his body through a syringe. But there was an additional report, included with the medical report, written by the ME investigator. She wrote in her report that my father was a recovering alcoholic. What? What on earth did this have to do with my brother's death in a locked facility? What she didn't include was that it had been over 20 years since my father had a drink. In fact, he stopped drinking before my brother was even born, so I'm not sure why she felt it was important to include, other than as an attempt to disparage my parents. To this day, I question her motivation.

She went on to write that the nurse assigned to watch my brother observed him holding his breath and in doing so questioned if his death could be ruled as a suicide. This is flat wrong on several points. Firstly, he was strapped down to a bed in a five-point restraint and he couldn't have done anything to harm himself. Secondly, you cannot hold your breath and die, and it is a sham to suggest breath holding equates to suicide. Any doctor will tell you that if you hold your breath long enough, your body will pass out and start regulating your breathing again. Our bodies are designed to maximize the chance of life with this involuntary reflex. In fact, the medical examiners piece of the report stated that the drugs not only caused the heart attack while he was prone restrained, but that it would have in a few short hours without the restraints. Essentially, they had already killed him and they didn't know it yet.

What is more shocking about her report is the admittance of negligence. She was implying that he was holding his breath and was therefore trying to take his own life. And the staff did nothing about it. That would be like a doctor witnessing a patient remove their breathing tube and continuing to walk past the door.

The week following Jeff's death was hectic from dealing with funeral arrangements and trying to figure out what and why this happened. The hospital handled the aftermath poorly. One of their managing staff members asked my parents to drive an hour to meet with him, instead of doing the right thing and reaching out to them. Within a few weeks, there were several more deaths in other parts of this hospital and JACHO came. JACHO is a non-profit on healthcare safety and stands for the Joint Commission on the Accreditation of Healthcare Organizations.

The JACHO report showed a failure to provide CPR to my brother even though there were several nurses and LVN's in the area. It also found that there wasn't even a crash cart in the psychiatric wing of the hospital. It showed a failure by the staff in keeping an eye on him at all times. JACHO threatened to remove the hospitals accreditation without making the required changes. But the changes would all come too late for Jeff.

There are times when your life completely diverges from its current path. Jeff's death was one of those times. What I knew as normal for 29 years of life, no longer was. I was now living a new normal. One in which there would be no new memories of Jeff.

~ ~ ~

After Jeff's death, my advocacy took on a new role. I wanted to understand how this could have happened in a place of healing and how I could prevent another loss of life. One mental health provider started a local workgroup to look into the use of seclusion and restraints in the County. I'm proud to say that all of the local hospitals became activate participants on this issue. In the wake of Jeff's death another mental health organization created the Jeffrey Christopher Award in order to honor individuals or organizations that are creating large impacts around stigma and discrimination. At the state level, NAMI California created the Zero Restraint Award.

Today, hospitals are an integral part of the mental health care system. Sometimes, the hospitals are used because there is simply a lack of other mental health treatment options. At other times, as was the case for Jeff, hospitalization is used as a threat for non-compliance with a treatment regime. Our goal should be that people seek out hospitals when they need them. Only as a last resort should people be handcuffed by a police officer, put in the back of a cop car, and forcibly taken to an inpatient psychiatric hospital. Once threats and coercion are used, trust in the system can diminish or disappear. When that happens, we all lose.

On top of that lack of trust, with the high levels of societal stigma and discrimination, it's easy to understand why mental health recovery is an uphill battle.

Many people will say to me, "but Shannon the stigma has been decreasing over time." Unfortunately, research does not support that statement.

Once I told one of my doctors that I run a mental health organization and we were about to put on a 5k WALK to raise money. He said to me, "so you are going to have a bunch of people running in strait jackets?" I was aghast.

Another example of stigma happened a few years ago when a hospital in a different state started discharging their mental health patients, without a care plan, and gave them bus passes to California. While I was being interviewed by the local media, the news reporter had been determined to get me to say, "Everyone needs to stay indoors because we are at a higher risk of danger due to the increasing numbers of psychiatric patients." The truth was far from that.

Alongside stigma creating a barrier to treatment is the reality that many people with a serious mental illness will die, on average, twenty-five years younger than the general population. At the time I was CEO of NAMI San Diego, one of my staff members was told by his psychiatrist that he had less than a year to live if he didn't do something about being so overweight. And yet, it was the prescribed psychotropic medicine that was causing him to gain weight.

At a conference where a psychiatrist spoke to a group of mental health providers, he posed the idea, "I would like everyone here to take a 100mg of Benadryl before you go to bed tonight and see what time you wake up in the morning." The reason he said this is because many of the treatment drugs cause people to sleep like cats, or roughly 16 hours a day. So if you don't take your meds you are considered non-compliant, but if you take them, you are considered lazy. Either way the patient can't win.

But even with the continuing stigma, I do see signs of progress. I see progress in awareness. People with mental illness are all over social media now, telling the world that they are here and that they will be heard. More and more men and women celebrities have taken on the mantel of mental health advocacy.

I also believe that siblings play a critical role in making change. Since we are not the parents who are often bogged down by time and resources, our combined voice can have a massive impact on stigma, policy, and the future of mental health care.

PART II

Sibling Stories

Chapter 11
Sibling Stories

Ellen

Siblings come in a variety of forms.

"Are you an only sibling?" I asked Ellen.

"Yes and no," she stated with a slight upturn of her lips.

Families come in all sorts of different shapes and sizes. Siblings can be whole, half-, and step-, and love binds them all together. There is a saying that the oldest child makes the rules, the middle child is the reason for the rules, and for the youngest, the rules don't apply. How would it affect you to go from being an only child to the oldest child of half-siblings, to the middle child with older step-siblings?

Ellen comes from a beautiful mixture of families. Her parents divorced and each re-married, adding both half-siblings and step-siblings. Her dad and stepmother produced two half-siblings, a brother and a sister. Her mom and stepfather added a baby girl who was fifteen years younger than Ellen and included two older and one younger step-siblings. For her, this made a total of seven children and two separate families. Even though she had a large family, she was also an island who was on her own, and she would oscillate between her parents' new families. "The bouncing between parents could be isolating at times," Ellen explained. "I didn't have a sibling to bounce with because I was an only child from my parents' union."

Mental illness and addiction would become well-known factors in both of her families, impacting her little brother on her dad's side, her little sister on her mom's side, and Ellen herself.

In her early twenties, Ellen was diagnosed with bipolar disorder. "My dad tried to be supportive but whenever I tried to bring up his own mental health he would shut down and change the subject." Ellen's voice held some anger behind her words. "I don't know if it was stigma, me, or what, but he didn't let me talk about it, and then, when I was twenty-four, my little brother took his life. It wasn't until after my brother died that my dad shared that my brother had been diagnosed with bipolar disorder four years prior."

This news impacted Ellen greatly. "What ifs" were still plaguing her. What if she had known about her little brother's diagnosis—could she have helped him? Had he needed a compassionate, listening ear who understood the ups and downs of a mental illness? Today, she is still working through her anger that her father didn't tell her about her brother's own diagnosis and never acknowledged Ellen's own battle with bipolar disorder—or her grief of losing a brother.

Meanwhile, on her mom's side, her little sister Ivy turned toward illegal drugs to deal with her mental health. Ellen would spend the next several years battling her own mental health condition and trying to "fix" her sister.

"Since I'm so much older than my sister, I've sometimes taken on the role of co-parent," Ellen said. It is typical for older siblings to take on the role of parent, even to the chagrin of the younger siblings.

Ellen continued, "Ivy's main issues are with drugs and alcohol. I had to learn more about what I could and couldn't control when someone is an addict. I found Al-Anon, and they have saved me and our relationship." Ellen pulled out her little Al-Anon book with the group's well-meaning and encouraging phrases to live by.

Her favorite quote is: "It is difficult to make a man miserable while he feels worthy of himself and claims kindred to the great God who made him" (Abraham Lincoln).

"What I love about Al-Anon is that groups are everywhere. I can go to a meeting while on vacation."

Today, Ivy is working toward get better. She is enrolled in a medication-assisted treatment program. She has a long road ahead of her, and Ellen is worried what could happen. She understands, however, that for both Ivy and herself, she has to take it one day at a time.

Ellen also explained that both she and her siblings have work to do on trying to forgive negative actions that have hurt all of them. She then said, "But I haven't really even allowed myself to think about that, because my default is to stay in the helper role. My brother isn't here anymore to be a part of that process… although I guess I could write him a letter. Perhaps I will do that. With my sister, who has a severe addiction, I feel that I need to wait for her to make amends. And because our relationship is in a holding pattern, she is not able to do that now. This is hard because I don't have control over that, and I'm not sure she will ever get to that place in her recovery."

Ellen adamantly stated that she does not include her sister in her personal mental health well-being plan. Then she said with a sigh, "I guess I feel like my sister can't handle being asked to do something. Perhaps I should reconsider including her so that she can feel the power dynamic shift… although, once again, I am thinking about what is helpful to her and not to me. Ugh! I'll give this some more thought."

Ellen enjoyed sharing her story; it gave her the safe space to talk about her siblings in ways no one has ever asked her. It allowed her to acknowledge that their struggles forced her to look at herself and her actions in a deeper way.

"I've had to consciously work to take responsibility for my thoughts and feelings related to what my siblings go through, and to find ways to also take care of myself in a conscious way (since my autopilot is to help them before helping myself)."

Ellen's advice to siblings:

- Practice journaling, because it allows you to acknowledge your experience for yourself. This helps you to be more open to the parts of the process that can happen naturally between you and your siblings. Sometimes expectations and previous experiences can get in the way of moving forward in your relationship with your siblings, and I think they can feel that. Some things you just have to do for yourself before you can ask for anything from them.

- Seek out groups like Al Anon and NAMI (National Alliance on Mental Illness).

- Practice self-care.

Carlos

Conflicts with parents can make sibling relationships stronger. "When your parents, who are the anchors you're counting on the most, are falling down on the job, siblings look to each other and find ways to pull together, because the last thing you can afford to see fractured at that point is the unit among yourselves."

~Jeffrey Kluger, author of *The Sibling Effect*,
in an interview with Salon Media Group.

What happens when the sibling who stepped into the role of parent by necessity—the person you look up to—develops a mental illness and tries to take her life?

On a Monday, even though it should have been like any other day, Carlos's big sister attempted to take her life. Depression and psychosis had been plaguing her for years but went unnoticed and misunderstood by her family and her youngest brother, who had been living with her. Their age difference was so great that, in many ways, he saw his sister as a second mother. At the time, his childhood home wasn't the safe, secure environment that it needed to be for a child to thrive, and his sister offered her home. Carlos went to live with her, her husband, and their three children. Carlos described his sister during those years as a beautiful, intelligent woman.

"She had this amazing smile," he said. However, the changes that he saw in his sister led to feelings of concern as well as frustration.

Carlos described himself during that time as confused, scared, and constantly questioning what was wrong with his sister. He felt like he was losing her, which made him angry with her. Because he wasn't even aware of mental illness, he did what most people do when symptoms of paranoia appeared—he assumed she was taking drugs.

But that Monday would force the family's eyes to open. His sister was a bus driver for the city. She loaded up passengers, drove them over a popular bridge, and promptly dropped off all of the passengers. She proceeded to drive the bus back across the bridge, then attempted to drive it off the bridge. Thankfully, she survived, and no one was hurt. The police took her to a mental health hospital. However, that was just the beginning. The media emerged, and they were all over the place. They were outside of the hospital reporting her every action, including her previous records and insights into her family, such as who they were and why she would do something so extraordinary. They exploited everyone to whom she was connected.

This young brother, who saw his sister as more of a mother, stood outside the hospital. His gaze was trained on the four-wall institution. Carlos was told by his brother-in-law that he could visit her. A part of him wanted to go in and check on her for himself, just to make sure she was alright. And then there was the other part of him, the winning part, that was angry, hurt, and disappointed. Why would she do that to him? He thought she loved him. Maybe she didn't. Maybe she loved only herself. That must be the case, right? Because she was willing to leave him and her family. She put her family in the eyes of the media and humiliated them all. Only the most selfish person would do that, right?

Years later, Carlos has grown into a man. He has served our country in the Iraq War, he has volunteered at an at-risk- youth organization, and he works daily to support individuals with disabilities to get back on their financial feet.

I asked him how his sister was today and inquired about the status of their relationship.

"She is missing," Carlos replied. "Over seven years ago, she stopped coming to family events, and I haven't seen her since." You can see both pain and anger warring with each other inside his mind. He wants his sister to be safe, but he isn't ready to talk with her.

After the Iraq War, Carlos has worked hard to maintain his own mental health. He experienced much emotional and physical pain. My question is, has a therapist ever asked Carlos how his relationship with his sister played a role in his own mental health?

When Carlos was asked what would have helped during those years, he responded with, "Family therapy would have helped. If not therapy, then education."

Carlos's advice for siblings:

- Don't be quick to judge.

- Don't pity your siblings with a mental illness.

- Know that functioning individuals are still there.

- Don't give up on your siblings. You don't want to end up creating so much distance that one day you don't even know what they look like anymore.

- Don't stop being a friend, and don't stop being a sibling.

- Whether you are the younger or older sibling, be there.

- Carlos's advice for parents:

- Reach out to mental health agencies.

- Don't be close-minded to the possibilities of what your child could be going through.

- Don't blow off that your child is just a teenager.

- Pay attention to and allow for expression of emotions, both ups and downs.

- Educate yourself on mental illness.

- Don't block yourself with your opinion.

- Prepare yourself to be that strong voice for your child.

Three Sisters: Suzy, Ellie, and Dani

"Close sibling relationships are good for your health. A Harvard University study showed that being close to one's siblings at college age was related to emotional well-being at age sixty-five. According to researcher Mark Morman of Baylor University, siblings who maintain close relationships in adulthood are less at risk for depression."

~Daniel Goleman

Suzy is the oldest of three sisters. While growing up, all three sisters were like peas in a pod. They would play together, dress the same, and pretend they were triplets. Over the years, they remained close but began to make their own friends and have different interests. They still were bonded by the activities of their youth and the annoyance of their parents.

Then one year, the middle sister, Ellie, began to act "strange.". She started ditching school, smoking marijuana, and dating a new boy every month. Her grades dropped and her interest in family affairs became non-existent. Their parents thought she was working through teenage hormonal changes. They would ground her, take away privileges, and pile on chores—but nothing worked. This mellow middle child went from being happy and friendly to expressing rage and deep sadness in a matter of minutes. Suzy, the older sister, was distressed by what she was seeing and experiencing but dealt with it on her own. The younger sister, Dani, became angry and distant. She refused to believe that Ellie couldn't control her behaviors.

As Dani explained it, "I felt like I was watching my parents turn into shells of their former selves, and it was all *Ellie's* fault. She could have chosen to seek help. And not just *seek* help but *listen* to what the doctors were saying."

Suzy, as the older sister, became the family caretaker. She alternated her time between the needs of her sisters and her parents, all of whom were now in crisis.

"My life became a blur of needs. I was worried that my mom and dad were slipping into a form of depression. My youngest sister was turning into a selfish pain. I admit, a part of me couldn't wait to go back to school in the fall, and yet, another part of me was scared to death to leave everyone alone."

Over the next six months, Ellie was in and out of several inpatient psychiatric hospitals. The parents had to take out a second mortgage on their home to pay for her bills. When Ellie was out of the hospital, she barely did more than lie in bed or find access to drugs. Her other two sisters became increasingly frustrated with her, with their parents, and then with each other. The younger one, Dani, didn't understand why everyone else wasn't forcing her sister to get her act together. She had heard the phrase "tough love." She believed her parents should kick her sister out of the house and force her to stand on her own two feet. By now, Ellie was in her twenties and old enough to have an independent life.

"She was like a blob, just lying in her bed all day, not doing anything," Dani sighed.

Suzy was equally frustrated, but her discouragement extended to the system in general. "It took months to get her into an appointment, and then follow-up appointments were always with a different person. How could my sister possibly get to a place of opening up to a therapist, if every week she had a new therapist? Plus, there is nothing out there for a young twenty-something. She needs to be around other young people who are going through the same thing she is."

A couple of years later, Ellie was finally in a good place. She was working part-time and taking some online classes. Her mood had stabilized, and some of the happy-go-lucky personality started to shine through.

"I would not be here today if it wasn't for my sisters," said Ellie with a slight blush. "I know things have been rough. Mental illness is no joke," she said. "Without my sisters, my parents, and my coach, I would still be on the couch. It felt like mental illness took away my identity, and now I'm slowly figuring out who I am again." Ellie carefully and nervously pats both of her sisters' hands.

Suzy is ecstatic, and Dani is happy, but both are scared that their sister will one day be in crisis again.

"It's a weird feeling to be both happy and scared out of your mind," Dani explained. "I love my sister, and I never want her to go through this again."

"Trust is something we are all working on," Suzy said. "But there is some kind of peace in the knowledge that if Ellie has a step backward, we've been there, done that," Suzy smiled. "We all have more knowledge and experience than when this first started." Suzy looked at her sisters for confirmation, and they all nodded their heads.

Tips from Suzy, Ellie, and Dani:

- Educate yourself. "Mental illness seemed to happen overnight. I felt like we were blindsided, and that scared us all," Suzy shared.

- Seek out therapy for yourself.

- Do something you used to do when you were kids, and not just with your siblings, but also with your parents.

- Get a coach. Ellie's family hired a peer coach to work with her. "The coach is a mixture of occupational therapist, social worker, and friend. We meet one-on-one each week, and somedays, just at the local coffeehouse," Ellie said.

Sharon

> "Our siblings push buttons that cast us in roles
> we felt sure we had let go of long ago - the baby,
> the peacekeeper, the caretaker, the avoider...
> It doesn't seem to matter how much time has
> elapsed or how far we've traveled."
>
> ~Jane Mersky Leder

Sharon is in her mid-forties, works part-time, and has a mental illness. Her older brother moved away from the family, but he and Sharon maintain their relationship—although it is somewhat stilted. She describes her parents as good people who have been married for fifty-two years. However, both of them had a hard time accepting that anything was wrong with her. She didn't know if they were ignoring her symptoms, didn't care enough, or simply didn't know what to do. Her mom had been dealing with anxiety and depression for years by drinking alcohol, but she never really talked about it. Sharon is proud to say that her mom has been sober for years now and that they are closer than ever.

When Sharon ended up in the psychiatric hospital for the first time, her dad wanted to control everything, as if this control would lead to her being cured. Instead, it caused a fissure in their relationship that has taken time to heal. Her brother became distant and never visited Sharon when she was in the hospital. And even though she became an adult, her brother kept treating her like a child. In fact, he pushed her parents into believing that she still was a child.

Over time, Sharon's brother did try to work on their relationship by sending her e-mails or occasionally taking her to the movies, but for the most part, he remained distant. He then married and had a family. While Sharon loves her sister-in-law, the feeling isn't recip-rocated, and Sharon believes that fear of being around a person with mental illness plays a role in this. Sharon has remained hopeful that eventually she will have a closer relationship with her brother and his family. She knows that, if she needs him, he will be there. She trusts him enough to have shared her WRAP "Wellness, Recovery, Action" plan with him. She also knows that actions on her part helped to create the distance between her and her brother. Now, her brother tries to take a step back when there are issues, and they talk about them.

Sharon's advice to siblings:

- Let your siblings know that you are open to talking about the situation. This helps to alleviate their misconceptions or assumptions.

- Remind your siblings that they can't always control their feelings either. Let them know it is okay to be angry.

- Tell your siblings that what they are feeling is okay and even understandable.

- Suggest that your siblings take a step back when necessary, but then reopen the dialogue when they are ready.

Pharoh

> "Younger siblings look up to their older brothers and sisters and thereby learn how to cope with difficult situations later in their lives. On the other hand, being role models to their younger brothers and sisters help the older siblings develop proper nurturing and skills of compassion that they wouldn't otherwise possess."
>
> ~Sharangee Dutta

I've known Pharoh for many years. There is almost an easy camaraderie between us because we are both the eldest sibling and are mental health advocates.

Pharoh is a forty-year-old male with what he likes to call drug-induced psychosis, or what he doesn't like to call schizophrenia. When he was ten years old, his mother married the man who would become

Pharoh's adoptive father. The union gave him a little brother named BJ. His little brother was his shadow in their youth and would always follow him around. Pharoh told me with a smile and a reminiscent looks in his eyes that his friends accepted BJ into their inner circle.

"In fact, all of my Facebook friends are also BJ's friends," Pharoh tells me with a smile. You can sense that he is proud of the fact that his friends care and respect his baby brother. As kids, Pharoh recalled them playing football in the hallway and, of course, the lava floor game! I think all siblings have played this game (where you can't touch the floor) in their youth. Because of their age difference, they didn't have many years to live in the same house. At age eighteen, Pharoh left his eight-year-old brother behind to join the army. Little did he know that only two and a half years later he would be coming back home.

While in the army, Pharoh started to notice that his thinking was a bit different than what he thought was considered normal. "The last thing I remember in the army is getting into a fight, which was over nothing in particular, and I ended up in the brig," Pharoh said, recalling the painful memory with a blush of embarrassment. "Then, when a guard walked by my cell, I told the man that I was thinking of every horrible thing I had ever done in my whole life." He felt like the world was caving in on him and that he was being pounded by each negative thought.

The guard's response was, 'Man, you need to talk to someone.' It was sound advice, but Pharoh received little help in seeking mental health treatment from the military, and he was originally given a dishonorable discharge. He spent the next twenty years in and out of jails and prisons, being homeless and hopeless.

BJ and Pharoh experienced a role reversal, where BJ became the older sibling, always asking if Pharoh needed anything, like a ride to an appointment, etc. The support of his little brother became one of the most valuable parts of Pharoh's mental health journey. Pharoh told me that there was never a time he didn't want his brother around, especially during the dark days of his prison stay.

"When you are on the inside, you are the bad person. Everyone here is a criminal in an orange jumper. So when your sibling comes to visit, it means the world. It makes you feel cared for—that you are not so horrible to be loved."

Due to the help of his mother and another mental health advocate, both of whom never stopped fighting for Pharoh, his military discharge was changed to "honorable." Now, twenty years later, he can access services through the Veterans Administration.

Pharoh's advice to siblings:

- Love your siblings and be understanding.

- If you can, be there in person.

- Let us, the siblings with a mental illness, help you as well.

- Let anger be a natural feeling. Accept it, feel it, address it.

Danielle

> "Children spend more time with their siblings than anybody else. Studies show that by the time a child is eleven years old, he or she devotes about 33 percent of available spare time to interaction with siblings—more than the amount of time spent with parents, friends, teachers, or even time spent alone."
>
> ~Jeffrey Kluger

Danielle and her brother Brian loved to ski and would go on weekends and after school. Danielle, being the big sister by five years, was proud of the fact that she taught her little brother to ski. Back then, their parents would drop them off at the mountain in the morning and pick them up in the evening. These are the happy memories Danielle holds onto today.

At the age of twenty-seven, Brian died by suicide at their family home.

Danielle had left home for college at the age of eighteen, leaving her thirteen-year-old brother at home. They maintained a close bond, but their relationship had to defy the odds of long distance. Her brother would fly out to Colorado, where Danielle was living after college, for visits, and Danielle would come home for holidays. However, as Brian got older, he'd start to worry about things that were beyond his control and began to struggle at school.

Danielle, who had studied mental health in graduate school and was working in the field of social work, pointed out some of the concerns she had to her parents—like how Brian couldn't seem to control his emotions or how he'd always choose the harder path in life. Teachers who loved Danielle as a student saw her brother as a troublemaker. What was tricky about Brian's mental health is that on the surface it looked like anger management problems. This was the type of problem that could easily be explained away and didn't appear to be the usual signs of depression. However, with anger management problems came impulsivity. These two combined were likely the catalyst to Brian's decision to end his own life.

Brian called Danielle just before the night he took his life. He said he was doing really well and told Danielle that he loved her. Something about the conversation didn't sit well with Danielle.

After Brian's death, Danielle shut down. Danielle was raising two of her own babies, working full-time and watching her parents fall apart while also putting off dealing with her own grief. She didn't have anyone else to talk to and felt like she didn't have time to grieve. There were days when she just wanted to talk with Brian. He had been her support and sounding board. He had been the one who'd helped her when she got into a disagreement with their mom. And now he was gone.

Danielle knew that she needed help. Her friends tried but simply didn't know what to do. She started compartmentalizing her needs and found that pushing the grief down only made things worse. She started to lose weight, felt empty, and was no longer enjoying life the way she once was. Eventually she made her way to a local suicide-loss survivors' group. However, this did not address the lack of sibling support. Therefore, being the go-getter and fixer, a natural for elder siblings, Danielle started a support group and continues to lead this group monthly, more than a decade later. Having the connection to other survivors, especially siblings, helps her to feel understood and not alone. Danielle found that losing a brother didn't seem the carry the same weight or understanding that a different type of loss would. For some reason, society doesn't think people suffer very much when they lose a sibling.

For her, the support group felt like a gift—a group of individuals who shared a similar life experience and didn't stigmatize the loss.

Danielle's advice to other siblings:

- See if there is a way to connect with other siblings.

- Talk to others who get you. Pain isn't often valued for siblings, and siblings can be seen as "just" lost. Be with others who have walked the journey."

Her advice to other parents:

- When one child has a mental illness, the composition of the family is no longer in balance. Be sure to give the other children space to be just the siblings.

Samantha

"Younger siblings tend to be more rebellious and extroverted. A study on 390 families conducted by the Leiden University in the Netherlands found that younger siblings were much more *aggressive and rebellious* as opposed to their older siblings. Younger siblings often feel the need to speak up for themselves and stand up to their older siblings in order to receive attention from their parents, thereby contributing to their extroverted and rebellious nature."

~Sharangee Dutta

Samantha told me her story through the slow leakage of tears running down her cheeks.

"He is still missing," she sobbed. "He's has been missing for more than fifteen years."

Her brother was diagnosed with everything under the sun, from bipolar disorder, to schizoaffective disorder, to addiction. His diagnosis without treatment didn't help his case. Only four days after being discharged from an in-patient hospital stay, her brother Riley disappeared.

"How could he stay away from us all this time?" she asked. The unspoken question was, "Why doesn't he love me enough to come home?"

Samantha and Riley had a fairly typical childhood. They were two years apart in age and raised in a suburban lifestyle. They grew up both loving and nagging each other. Samantha couldn't recall a time when they had a major argument, but they did begin to grow distant when Riley started hanging out with his friends and smoking pot. She let him know that she didn't approve of his friends or his use of drugs. Her words didn't seem to deter him, which contributed to the distance between the two siblings.

Samantha went to college but stayed close to home. Riley, who had been a "straight A" student until his senior year, barely graduated from high school.

"My parents were pretty hard on him and tried to force him to get his act together; they practiced 'tough love'—you know what I mean," she said with an eye roll. And yes, I did know. "They figured if he hit rock bottom then his life would finally get back on track." But it never got back on track. Riley went from sleeping on one friend's couch to another, just to wear out his welcome. Everything changed for the worse when he started using meth. Even friends from high school who would sit around smoking pot with him now abandoned him.

"Everyone assumed that if things got bad enough, he would miraculously wake up one day and get clean and sober on his own."

Riley would spend the next few years homeless, in jail, or in a hospital.

"It was like he was spiraling down a rabbit hole with no way out." Samantha had a far-off look in her eyes, one that was full of unspoken guilt and pain.

"The last time I spoke to him, he showed up at my house asking for money." Samantha took a deep breath. "I gave him a couple of bucks and told him to get help." A few days later he was placed into a detox center and then a hospital. Samantha didn't visit. She was angry with him and let those feelings dictate her actions.

That hospital stay was the last time they knew where Riley was. Today, her family still has no idea where Riley is.

"We don't know if he is alive." A single tear pools up on her eyelid. "That's the hardest—not knowing." The tears drop again.

Samantha's advice to siblings:

- Say "I love you." You don't know if it will be the last time you can say it to that person.

- Make time. Your life is busy and important, but so is your family. Be there.

- Be an advocate. Question doctors, therapists, and pharmacists. You know your loved one better than anyone.

Alice

Twins: Born Together, Friends Forever

More than forty years ago, fraternal twins, Alice and Tom, were born. Like many twins, their childhood was full of togetherness. They experienced a sense of never being apart and of always being there for one another. There is a saying that the best gift your parents can give you is a sibling, and Alice and Tom surely felt that way.

In high school, Alice tried hard to get straight A's. Tom didn't need to try and got them anyway. Alice had dreams for the future, while Tom couldn't define his future. After high school, Alice moved away from their family's hometown for college and her career, and Tom followed with no sense of purpose. They lived in the same city but had separate apartments. Alice was always busy and became frustrated and angry because Tom couldn't figure out what to do with his life. She asked herself why wasn't he doing normal young-adult things, like going to school, getting a job, etc.

Then she started getting calls from landlords and neighbors. It almost became a full-time job keeping Tom from being evicted from his apartment and, when he did get evicted, finding him a new place. She knew something was wrong but was confused about what it could be. When she suggested he see a psychiatrist, Tom refused. One time when she visited Tom's apartment, he had smeared feces on the walls. Hiring a housekeeper was just one more bill she was paying to help Tom.

In the middle of the night, Alice received a phone call from Tom's latest landlord reporting that there had been a gunshot. Tom had shot the gun in the middle of the apartment for no apparent reason. When he was questioned why he had fired the gun, his response was, "It was there, and I decided to shoot it."

Alice loved her brother more than anything, but she was feeling worn out and tears became her constant companion. Her parents didn't offer any help, and they lived 3,000 miles away. Her brother's struggles really weren't a topic of conversation at happy hour with her friends. She felt she would never find a life partner who would love her when she had a brother with a mental illness. She felt alone.

Over the last decade, Alice did marry and have children of her own. During that time, her brother's health was a roller-coaster ride, and he has never really accepted having a mental illness. Employment for Tom was elusive. He would get a job, only to eventually be terminated.

"He is not in a place where he could live independently without my assistance, and this causes some tension between my husband and me," Alice shared.

Today, she still feels overwhelmed with taking care of her family and her brother, but she is more vigilant in taking care of herself. Alice started to see a therapist. She created some boundaries and structure around her relationship and caretaking of her brother. She started going to a gym, swims three days a week, and has even made some new friends.

"I'm a better mother, wife, and sister by taking caring of myself first," Alice said. "I will be my brother's caregiver for the remainder of our lives; therefore, I need to be the healthiest me I can be."

Alice's advice for siblings:

- You can't do it all alone. Delegate to others.

- Go to counseling for yourself.

- You are not alone. Find a support network.

Trudy

> "Siblings fight. A lot. Sometimes with a conflict every 10 minutes. Any parent of more than one child knows that they sometimes just don't get along. Whether it's a power struggle, competitive personalities or just plain irritation from being around one another, siblings spend a lot of time battling it out. One researcher found that brothers and sisters between 3 and 7 years old engage in conflict 3.5 times an hour. Younger kids fight even more, with a fight happening every 10 minutes."
>
> ~Nursing Schools.net

Trudy, Jared, and Levi grew up together in the 1980s, but when Trudy was asked to recall happy memories with her younger siblings, she could only reflect on her relationship with her youngest brother Levi. Jared was the harbinger of painful memories. She could only remember his constant taunting and belittling of her and how this emotional abuse affected her growing-up years. In fact, she remembers hearing stories about the bond of sibling relationships and wondered if she was an oddity for not sharing this special closeness with Jared. While she felt fondness toward Levi, she felt empty toward Jared, as if she was forced to know him because they shared the same parents. She remembered telling her parents about Jared's behavior—that he was a bully and she was his favorite target—but her parents simply told her that he was different and therefore she needed to be the bigger person and not take his words personally.

As an adult, she can reflect back that Jared's behaviors were a result of a mental health condition, but that didn't mean she wasn't affected by those behaviors. Nor did it mean that she shouldn't have been protected from his abuse. It wasn't right that Jared could get away with saying anything he wanted to blurt out.

Throughout the years, Trudy learned to distance herself from Jared—to simply not be around when he was there. But because his needs were greater than hers, by staying away from Jared, she also distanced herself from her parents, whom she did need—although at the time she couldn't admit it.

To this day, she still doesn't have a relationship with Jared and is not sure she ever will.

"I have realized that I'm not just dealing with the trauma of the past, but with grief over what has never been or ever will be."

Trudy's advice to siblings:

- Distance doesn't fix the emotional problems. Seek support.

- Mental illness is not an excuse for abuse. Speak up.

- It's okay to put yourself first. You are not the parent, and it's not your job to "fix" your siblings.

Nicole

"A good sibling relationship is excellent medicine for dealing with the terrible things in life."

~Dr. Jonathon Caspi

But what if one of your siblings has a mental illness? How do you deal with the terrible things in life if your support person is one of those "things?"

I sat down with Nicole at a coffee shop to interview her about her life's journey as a sibling to a brother who has schizoaffective-bipolar disorder. She had a warm, gentle smile. Her outward appearance would never suggest the pain and trauma she has suffered over the years.

At the age of five, Nicole was just a little girl who became the head of the household when she lost her father to suicide. Her mother had also recently passed away. Within a year, her family of four had been reduced to just herself and her three-year-old little brother. With the death of her parents, her father's brother and wife took care of her and her brother John. While technically they are her aunt and uncle, Nicole refers to them as Mom and Dad. Two years after relocating to live with her new parents, another baby boy was added to the family.

Nicole sighed as if she was questioning whether or not to continue sharing her story. "I love my mom and dad," she prefaced, "but they had a hard time raising the family."

While John and Nicole felt love in their new family, they didn't feel safe and secure. The family had continuous financial issues that forced them to move from place to place in order to avoid the inevitable eviction notice. Her mom stayed at home to raise the three children, but she became addicted to opioids and then continued to supplement her needs with illegal drugs. Her dad was a mechanic who worked constantly to make ends meet, but he was never at home to meet the emotional needs of the family.

Nicole worked hard, both academically and in various jobs. At a young age, she became a primary source of income for her family. On her heels, her brother followed her footsteps and started to work at a local bank. For a while, everyone was happy and healthy, and things seemed to be going okay. Nicole started dating a boy with whom she still lives today, eight years later. John started dating a girl who also worked at the bank.

In retrospect, mental illness blindsided the family. Their utopia was shattered by the introduction of paranoia. John started feeling like everyone was talking about him and that the government was watching him. There was an unfortunate mix up with a safety deposit box that led to John's termination, but he felt sure that he had been set up. He then became engrossed in a wrongful-termination lawsuit.

John's life turned into a roller coaster of employment, termination, homelessness, and mental health appointments. In the middle was Nicole—not her parents. She took care of scheduling John's medical appointments, chauffeuring him there and back, and spending her money on his medical needs as well as on the rest of the family. At one point, a facility tried to deny John access to mental health treatment, and together he and Nicole fought for what he needed.

John ended up at an inpatient psychiatric hospital, and during his stay there, his live-in girlfriend and daughter moved out of their apartment. Nicole felt that she had to mediate their issues and ensure that her niece remained a part of her and John's life.

As Nicole described it, she was the parent, care manager, lawyer, sister, and marriage counselor to her two adoptive parents and her brother—way too many roles. Looking away from me, Nicole said, "I only wanted to be the sister and the daughter, but how can I say 'no' to them?"

Saying "no" is difficult for so many caregivers, and yet, if you don't, you will become worn down and eventually will resent the people you are caring for. Fortunately, Nicole has a support person in her life. Her boyfriend has been her only safeguard. He doesn't encourage her to divorce herself from the needs of her family, but he also gives her the strength to say "no."

After our interview, Nicole was heading to her job and then later that night buying her brother and parents groceries. But tomorrow she had plans with her boyfriend.

What struck me the most while interviewing this young woman was her radiance. She loved her family and was willing to give of herself to ensure her brother had a chance at recovery. It was also clear throughout the interview that John made a point to continually let her know that he loved her. That ongoing message of love and thanks from her brother is what keeps her going. Even with all that she has given up to provide for her family, she says she will never give up on her brother. And I believe her.

Nicole's advice for siblings:

- Fight for your siblings. The mental health system is pretty messed up, and your siblings need you by their side in order to get the right treatment.

- Don't let the needs of your family consume you.

- Feel hopeful that recovery is possible.

Andrew

Older siblings are your first superhero.

But what if your sibling has done something unforgivable?

Andrew's story starts out in a suburban coastal county in the 1980s. While the other sibling stories are written as a result of an interview, I felt that it was best to leave Andrew's story in his own words.

Tell me about your family.

Growing up was pretty "normal" I suppose. We had a large family of 6 in which I am the youngest of four siblings. My sister is the oldest who is six years older than I. Next is my brother who is not only deaf and mute, but also has schizophrenia. He is five years older than me. Then, my other brother who is exactly one year older than me. We all attended school, played sports, and did family vacations. I never really thought twice about my brother's deafness. To me, it was normal. It was all I knew. In hindsight, I realize that I never really grasped or even attempted to understand what it may feel like to be deaf. From as little as I can remember, there is one thing I'm completely sure of. I always looked up to my brother. He was my idol. Being deaf and "different" never registered with me. Or maybe it did but I just thought it didn't matter. After all, he's my brother and I love him. He was a very athletic, strong and cool guy. I remember all the girls liking him and saying how good looking he was. Just another reason why I idolized him. As a young boy, there really wasn't anything he couldn't do. Whether it was sports, skateboarding or even dressing like him. To me, he was my older brother who I adored.

Everything was pretty normal up until I was about twelve years old and my brother had just graduated high school. The summer following my brother's high school graduation, he went back to New Jersey to work construction with my uncle. It was upon his return from the summer away, that I think the entire family noticed a difference. For me personally, I recall exactly when I noticed a difference in him. I specifically remember being extremely excited to have him come home. I hadn't seen him for three months. I was so excited that I left my friend's house in the neighborhood to race home and greet him. To my surprise, he didn't show any excitement whatsoever. I remember feeling disappointed that he wasn't as excited as I was to have him home. From that point on for the next two years, it was progressively downhill. My brother's behaviors started changing little by little. It's hard to really articulate and find words for his behavior. Knowing what I know now, I guess I would say it was the onset of depression and his schizophrenia. Nothing seemed to make him happy or excited. His outlook on life in general seemed pessimistic or negative. His friends stopped coming over and he left the house less and less. Eventually it reached the point of him never leaving the house and never having friends over anymore. It reached the point of him locking himself in his bedroom for close to 24 hours a day. The only time he came out was to get water and food. I recall water being the only thing he would drink. I also remember him saying that the reason he only drank water was because he was trying to cleanse himself. Not like health cleanse. A cleanse in the sense that he was trying to flush any impurity out of himself. It was a metaphoric cleanse in a sense. He started defecating and urinating in bottles and buckets in his room. He wouldn't even use the toilet. He gained an immense amount of unhealthy weight and refused to shave his face or get a haircut. He was almost be unrecognizable. He went from being a very physically fit, athletic and charismatic young man, to extremely unhealthy, overweight and depressed young man.

The next behavioral changes I recall were more activity based. There was one instance in which I recall coming home one day and my brother was on the roof. When it was inquired about, his response was something along the lines of him believing he was tele-pathically communicating with friends and/or voices. Furthermore, when the family would be gone for the day (at school or work), we would return home to a completely re-arranged household. For example, he would move all the furniture from a bedroom (or any other room) upstairs to the living room downstairs and vice versa. This happened time and time again. At night, he would sometimes go outside when everyone else was sleeping and decorate cars with toilet paper and other miscellaneous items. He even painted the entire garage one time with very weird cartoon like artwork. I think now that it was an expression of the internal mental battle he was having day in and day out.

As time went on, I remember my brother becoming increas-ingly paranoid. One day I came home from school and was home all alone with my brother. I remember he cornered me while on the balcony that protruded from my parent's bedroom. He was in an extremely agitated state as his body language and facial expressions told me so. He started physically grabbing my arms and forced me to look into his eyes while he asked me questions. He asked me questions like "what does he (my sister's boyfriend at the time) say about me"? Or "Is he talking bad behind my back"? Questions of that nature. Again, it was very paranoid thinking considering the questions he was asking held no validity. They were all fabrications of his own mind. I remember actually being scared for my physical well-being. I had called my sister to come pick me up. When my sister got there, I ran out to her car so we could leave. My brother chased us out into the street where he literally jumped up and kicked himself through the windshield of the car. Fortunately, we were able to drive away with no more damage being done and no one got hurt. Lastly, I recall one day he ran head first through a double plated glass door. He just paced around the backyard with an angry face and blood dripping down his body.

The last thing I want to share speaks more to the paranoia he had. I remember at night he would walk around the house with a knife while looking out the windows and doors. When I asked him what he was doing, he always replied with "They're out there" and "I'm keeping us safe". He never elaborated on who "they" were. He just felt like someone(s) was always after him or our family. Despite all my brother's weird behaviors and actions, I firmly believe that he kept his family's safety a priority. I feel all of his actions that were based on his paranoia, stemmed from wanting to keep our family safe.

All these instances only increased in severity and nature. Up to the event that changed our family's and other's life as we knew it. Without going into too many details, there was one summer night that I will never forget. My entire family was home except for me. I was out with friends and trying to meet up with my girlfriend when I received the daunting call from my other brother. He was in tears and crying hysterically. I couldn't make out what he was saying to me. Finally, he gathered up enough composure to tell me the words I'll never forget. He informed me that our brother had stabbed our neighbor. I remember being brought home that night around midnight, immediately after I received the phone call. I came home to my entire street lit up with lights from all the ambulances, fire trucks and police cars. I don't remember too many details other than one police officer telling me he was unsure if the victim was going to make it. I remember seeing both my parents in their underwear and bed clothes, covered in blood from trying to help our neighbor who had been stabbed. The victim didn't make it and was pronounced dead. My brother spent two years in the county jail while he awaited his trial. After the trial, he was moved into a state hospital to get the help he needed. He spent roughly twelve years in the state hospital getting the treatment he so desperately needed over a decade before.

What was your reaction to your brother's changes in behavior?

To some degree I think I ignored it as much as possible. I was a young boy that was trying to find his own way through life. I don't even think I knew what schizophrenia or any other mental diagnosis was at the time. Additionally, I was somewhat angry and frustrated at times. I was frustrated that I had to deal with his fabricated accusations and paranoia.

I remember making excuses or laughing at his behavior when friends were around. I was too caught up in my rebellious teenage years to really understand what was happening with him. To some degree, I was too immature to realize that anything serious was taking place. It was all semi slow and progressive. It's not like we woke up one day and he was different. It got worse and worse over time. Little by little. To the point that what happened, happened. It wasn't really until then that the harsh reality set in and I had to learn how to deal and cope with things in my own unhealthy ways. By acting out with violence myself and drug/alcohol abuse. By that point, the entire family was basically trying to deal with all the emotions and repercussions on an individual basis. We never expected anything like that to happen. Our entire lives were turned upside down at the drop of a hat.

Do you have a relationship with your brother today? Do you have any limitations on the relationship?

Yes I have a relationship with him but there are some restrictions due to his program with CONREP. He lives with my parents who live in a different county. That coupled with the fact that I have started my own family a few years ago, time is limited to spend with him. I do invite him to do things with me though. I went skydiving with him, went dirt bike riding with him and attempt to exercise with him from time to time. I definitely understand the importance of family involvement. To be totally honest, I wish I had the ability to spend more time with him than I do. I feel like he really needs it. He gets sad and upset and feels like no one like him if we're not actively trying to spend time with him.

Do you feel your parents contributed to your relationship with your brother or sister today?

Absolutely. My parents always pushed us to be involved in his life, especially after the major life changing event. I'm not sure what kind of a relationship I would have with my brother if any had it not been for my parents. They led by example and their actions spoke louder than their words. I can't speak for my siblings but for me, my parents are saints for their examples and perseverance over the last decade and half.

Did you find yourself needing your parents more from your stress of the situation?

In hindsight, yes. At the time, no. I thought all I had to do what be a tough guy. Truthfully, I was a scared young boy. I didn't know how to deal with that fear other than be defensive and angry. I remember telling myself things like "I won't get hurt again and I'll hurt someone before they hurt me". I also feel that I was at least mature enough to know I didn't want to burden my parents with anything. I never intentionally did anything to hurt my parents after the life changing event. My actions would have said otherwise but it was never intentional and I know that. Seeing my parents hurt the way they did was enough to know that they didn't need any extra burden. Maybe that's why I never asked for help. I think I was too prideful to admit I was scared and sad and angry. Or maybe I was just too scared to say I was scared.

Were you frustrated by your parents? Did you feel that they were giving your sibling too much attention?

I personally never felt that way. My other siblings may have, but I didn't. I always just wished I could help alleviate some of my parents pain and suffering. Don't get me wrong. There were some points where I wanted to tell my parents "I'M YOUR CHILD TOO"! but I always knew where the importance was. The simple truth was my brother needed it more than the rest of us. It was just a matter of being mature enough to recognize that. It wasn't' until I got my act together at twenty-four years of age that I finally realized that completely.

What advice would you give other parents and siblings?

Seek help! There is absolutely no shame in it. Seek other parents and families in the same or similar positions. Seek families/individuals that have similar experiences. I've learned that support groups and being able to relate with others that have similar experiences, can be some of the best forms of therapy. Don't forget that your family is a priority. They need to feel that way. Specifically, other children. They need attention and to know they are important. Life changing events and mental illness in general can destroy a family faster than anything I've seen. Be prepared to fight for what matters - your family. In my experience, it's been a long, tiresome road and it's still not over. It never will be. I feel parents need to be prepared for a life-long run of catering to others because they need it more. But I also would want other parents to know that it's all worth it. And lastly, finding and leaning on faith/God/Religion/Higher power should be considered – in my humble opinion. The road to recovery is LONG and trying. There are many ups and many downs. The highs are high and the lows are low. Take all the help you can get.

Do you worry about what will happen when your parents are gone? Do you have a plan?

Yes. My parents are still the caretakers for my brother who is sick. He lives with them, he relies on them. When my parents are gone, I have a feeling that I will be the one to care for my brother the most. Depending on how far he evolves up to that point will be a contributing factor to how much care he will need from family. I don't have a plan because I don't know what kind of help he will need down the line. He is still recovering, learning and navigating his way through life considering he was locked up in jail and hospitals for his entire adulthood. There's still so many things for him to learn between technology, finding a job, and just basically how to be an adult and a productive member of society. What I do know is this.... I'm prepared to care for him no matter what it takes.

Anything else?

Keep in mind mental illness is treatable. My simple advice is this... Find support groups, make your family a priority and find some sort of faith if you don't already have it.

PART III

Loss, Love, and Healing

Chapter 12
When the Light Extinguishes

"Grieving is like having broken ribs. On the outside
you look fine, but with every breath, it hurts."

~Author Unknown

This chapter is about sibling loss. It can be read separately from the rest of the book and is broken into topic segments. I delve into grief and it's sudden return. I talk about the dreaded annual date of loss and the wavering belief in faith when a sibling dies. Lastly, I talk about comfort and healing.

Sibling loss is unique. I hope this chapter does justice to the rollercoaster of emotions you have experienced since the loss of your sibling that maybe no one has ever asked you about.

Grief

When your sibling dies, you lose a part of your past, present, and future, and one of your most compassionate friends.

My mother said that I became a second mommy at the ripe age of four, which was the moment my brother was placed in my arms. As he grew, naturally he had to follow *my* rules. I was the oldest. Need I say more?

I remember when he first came to kindergarten and I was in third grade. I would watch the kindergarten playground to make sure he was okay and that no one was teasing him. I taught him how to tie his shoes, to sneak candy, and how to be daring. It seemed like from the moment he learned to walk, I'd find him coming into my bed at night. I always made sure though, to take the side of the bed by the wall, because Jeff was a mover and I didn't want to fall off! On Christmas mornings, I was the one who kept him entertained by grabbing our stockings and giving my parents some extra time to sleep.

I had dreams for our future. I wasn't surrounded by cousins growing up and decided that Jeff and I would have kids at the same time and create a larger family for our children. I, of course, would have to approve of whomever he married. Remember—I was the oldest.

Siblings may take different paths and life may separate them, but they will forever be bonded by having begun their journey in the same boat.

A few years ago, my husband and I were about to put on a movie when my mother called. She was talking to my husband, but I could hear her screaming with tears. After he hung up, he looked at me and said, "Jeff was killed." In one moment, with one phone call, the world tilted. For everyone else, the world keeps going, but when your brother or sister dies, so does a piece of you. My brain couldn't rationalize my husband's words. He knew I was planning to visit my brother the next day; therefore, *Jeff couldn't be dead.*

Grief isn't reserved just for the parents. I have often felt that people asked me how I was doing as an afterthought. What my parents, and all parents who have lost a child, have gone through is the most unimaginable loss. As a mom, I never want that experience. But Jeff was gone, and I lost my best friend—my past and my future. Siblings deserve to be asked, "How are you today?" In fact, grief is unique to each person, and loss comes in many different forms.

When my brother died, I didn't just lose a brother—I lost an uncle for my children, a caretaker for aging parents, a part of my team. I lost the person who held the memories of my childhood—a person who could embarrass me by telling my husband stories of the past. I lost a piece of me. And when you lose a piece of yourself, it doesn't just heal. You learn to adjust without it.

For me, the hardest thing is looking at pictures and knowing I have memorized every single one that will ever exist with Jeff in them. The years of new pictures and memories will not include him. But then my daughter smiles, and while she will never have met her uncle, she carries a piece of him in her smile. In that moment, I have a new memory of my brother.

For all of you who have lost a sibling, no matter how young or old, or when you suffered your loss, let me ask, how are you doing?

When Grief Unexpectedly Resurfaces

When my parents almost lost my childhood home in a wild-fire that swept through our neighborhood the grief of losing my brother unexpectedly returned. Fortunately, their house was spared, while their neighbors' was not. The fire broke out miles away from their home on a Thursday afternoon—far enough away to put them on alert but not alarm them. We continued to watch the trajectory of the fire, the direction of the winds, and the number of personnel available to put out the fire before damage was done. Factors beyond anyone's control were not in favor of the fire being put out. Humidity remained in the single digits, the land hadn't received any rain in months after a dry summer, and the wind was fanning the flames. Within a few short hours, my parents had to evacuate.

I was on a work trip and keeping tabs from afar. Mentally I was pulled in two directions—concern for my parents and their home, and the task in front of me. By Thursday night the fire reached their front and back doors. Hope was losing the battle.

Every emotion I experienced from the moment my brother was diagnosed to the day he died came rushing back. The feeling of helplessness took root once again. Should I fly home or stay put? As someone who knows her own mind, I slipped back into wanting someone else to give me direction, and I felt starved for information. What was happening? And why could no one stop it from happening?

Thursday night I went to bed with the very real possibility that my childhood home would be gone. A part of me was angry at myself for being emotional about a "thing" that could be replaced, especially when I knew the pain of losing a brother. But it wasn't just the home that I was grieving over—it was the loss of my brother once again. Let me be clear, a home is not just a "thing." It is a place of love, memories, warmth, and security. There are many reasons why people love coming home, even after a great vacation. My family even had plans to go to my parents' house on Sunday. We were taking the kids and going to stay the night; so, the house had to be standing, right? All the feelings from when I received that fateful call from my mom about Jeff's death came rushing back to me. My brain had vehemently denied the loss of Jeff, because I was supposed to visit him the next day. And now, I was denying that my parents' house could possibly be lost. It is hard to realize that the plans you make can be forever changed in an instant.

A week after the fire, I came across a stranger's post on Facebook about the loss of his brother. He described the frantic call from his mother, the hasty drive in the car to get to his parents' home, and the excruciating need to figure out what had happened and to confirm the truth. Even though you know your parents wouldn't lie, a part of you holds onto the hope that they heard it wrong. And once again, I flashed back to everything from the night my brother was killed. Now, since I've been on the other side of loss for some time, I react to the painful journey of healing that he and his family are now on. I have a deep understanding and shared grief, not just for the loss of his brother, but also for the loss of who he was before he received that phone call.

For all of us who have received that phone call, this story may take you back to that moment. If it does, it's important to let yourself cry and grieve. Protect yourself as well. Don't take on another sibling's grief. No matter what, I cannot take away the pain this other young person is going through, and it doesn't do anyone any good for me to go back to those initial moments of loss.

We may think we have a good handle on our grief, and in many ways we probably do, but that doesn't mean that our grieving is over. Just like the initial loss can happen suddenly, so can triggers spike your grief once again. *There is no time limit on grief.* People sometimes act as if the only thing that happened was that you "lost" your brother or sister, and as if it were something you would get over in a few days or weeks. And even "unspoken" words can make you feel like you should be over it, that somehow losing your sibling was a "minor" loss, whatever that means. I personally don't prescribe to "minor" losses. A loss that is meaningful to you is a significant loss, no matter who or what it is. And there is definitely nothing "minor" about losing a sibling.

Healing from grief is a journey, not a destination. Depending on where you are in this journey, I hope you have a good day, hour, or moment—and know you are not alone.

Dealing With "Angelversaries"

"You will always be like a handprint on my heart."

Let me take a moment to talk about the date that comes around every year like clockwork—a date you cannot hide from. You can't bury it like other aspects of grief, because no matter what, the date will appear each year.

Every year on April 11, is what I call the "angelversary" of the day my brother was killed. "Angelversary" is a term coined to denote the annual date for the passing of a loved one. Some people say "sadiversary" or "remembrance day." Personally, I'm not in love with any of these terms, and as one support group grief survivor said, "There are just not many words to adequately describe grief."

An angelversary is not a celebration. No one says, "happy anniversary." In fact, after a few years, no one says anything at all. But I remember the day like it was yesterday. Just writing these words takes me back to that moment when my life was altered forever.

The hushed words that Jeff had been killed and the moments afterward make me feel as if time itself has stopped and that it plays on repeat like a broken record.

This day confronts me every year. I usually get irritable in March, and for some time I wasn't attuned to why this happened. I recall noticing that around my brother's third year of passing, something was off. I then realized that I began to grieve his loss again—but several weeks before the actual date. Once I figured this out, I understood that I had to take some extra self-care steps and even plan more time for me to be alone. On April 11, I always spend the day by myself. I don't work. I don't go out. I don't go to the gravesite. I put on a movie or read a book. This might sound odd, but for me it actually feels peaceful. The days leading up to April 11 are what actually cause me anxiety.

Once I lost my brother, I was immersed in a new society of people who had suffered losses. Each person spends the angelversary of his or her loved one in a different way. For example, my parents find solace at my brother's gravesite. Some people go to the cemetery to feel closer to their loved one and speak to them. For me, the gravesite is a confirmation of his passing, and I don't visit it often. I prefer to talk to my brother when I'm alone or through stories with other people. We all cope with our grief in ways that feel right for us.

You probably already have your own ritual for your loved one's angelversary, but here are a few ideas:

- Write a letter to your loved one.

- Visit the gravesite (if it feels right for you).

- Do something you used to enjoy doing together, like watching a favorite movie, going to the beach, or listening to a song.

- Share a story with someone about your loved one's life.

- Plant an annual flower, light a candle, or place a rock in remembrance of your loved one.

Whatever you choose to do, do it not out of guilt, but because it feels right for you.

On April 11 this year you will find me at home, alone, watching a movie that my brother and I used to love as kids. But I reserve the right to change my mind and do something else if that feels right. This is my grief, and grief is nothing if not personal.

I have often found that other friends and family members don't know what to do on these angelversaries. They usually remember the date but are unsure of what actions to take. Doing nothing is probably the worst. After talking to other grieving families, here are some tips to support someone through their loved ones' angelversary.

- **Remember the date.** No matter how many years have passed, we will never forget the day our loved one passed away. It means the world to us that you've remembered it as well. We know that, for you, it may be a nondescript day, but for us, it is profound. Showing that you remember can come with a simple text: "Thinking about you today." "You and your brother are in my thoughts today." It doesn't have to be anything fancy, but a simple reaching out between friends makes a great deal of difference to us.

- **Share something about our loved one.** If you knew your friend's loved one, share a story. We love hearing about them. It keeps them alive. Yes, the story can bring tears to our eyes, but we still want to hear them.

- **Use their name.** People tend to shy away from those who are grieving, but even more upsetting is that they don't utter the name of the person who passed. Our loved ones are not Voldemort. The saying, "He who shall not be named," doesn't apply to those who are grieving. In fact, while you may be assuming that hearing our loved one's name will cause us to grieve more, it actually has the opposite effect. Names are very powerful. They give life to our loved ones.

- **Do something that our loved one enjoyed doing.**
  Personally, I like to be alone on Jeff's anniversary, but
  some people like to hang out with a group of friends who
  were their loved one's friends as well. This can be a very
  meaningful time.

- **Don't try to make us feel better.** I know this is hard, and
  it is advice that may go against the grain. But let us simply
  talk while you listen. Laugh with us, and when we cry, let
  us cry. If you don't know what to say, just sit there. Simply
  being there and connecting with us can be the greatest
  gifts of support.

Sibling Loss and Faith

When a brother or sister dies, your faith will be tested and retested.
Many times, your faith is left hanging perpetually in midair. At least,
that is the way it has been for me. Before my brother was killed,
I was a regular churchgoer. Yes, I had my doubts, but I cherished
having a belief in God. In fact, when I was a little girl, I was an
altar server. I loved serving the Lord, not to mention the fact that
mass went a lot faster when you had something to do!

While there can be much angst in religion, there can be much
peace in belief. To believe in the afterlife is to know that your loved
one is in a better place. You can still miss that person like you are
missing an arm, but you can do so with a smile because you know
that he or she is happy and that one day you will see your loved
one again. But for me, losing my brother made me question all of
my beliefs. Was he really somewhere else, happy, healthy, smiling
down at me and laughing because he was somewhere better off
than I was? Or was he gone, leaving behind a shell of a body? A
body that will be buried and never be seen again? A body that will
never know light, a heart to never beat, a mouth to never speak? I
honestly don't know. It's been years since my brother's passing, and
I wish feverishly that I could go back to the beliefs I had once held.

I would love to feel secure in the knowledge that Jeff is somewhere and that his twenty-five years on Earth weren't his only time of existence. But I'm not.

Loss can make you question your beliefs. Once you've have experienced a loss like this, you enter into a new family of people who experienced similar losses. Each person I have met over the years has questioned his or her faith. Some seem to be closer to God than ever before, some have walked away from Him completely, and others (like me) are still questioning and not feeling resolved in their faith.

Like grief, faith is personal. Our relationship with faith, spirituality, and God is all personal. When we decided to baptize our girls, I knew that I couldn't participate in the one-hour teaching session on faith at our local parish, because it was most likely being taught by a person whose life was untouched by the pain we've experienced. We were very fortunate to find a deacon that understood this and came to our house instead. This seemingly simple act has brought me closer to my faith again and has allowed me to feel peace in teaching my children about God.

My Comfort Place

When you grieve, you also need to find comfort. For some it is in faith; others find it in support groups or therapy. Others still may become involved in special causes. I have found it in books.

When my brother was killed, I had already spent numerous years as a mental health advocate. I had supported many family members in reaching out to therapists and other providers in their time of need. You would think that, during my own time of need, I would have taken that same approach. Well, I did. And let's just say it didn't work for me. I have always believed that a person's journey to mental wellness is personal and different for each person. Therapists and licensed professionals have been miracle workers for some individuals but not for others. Formalized sessions around cognitive behavioral therapy (CBT) and dialectical behavioral therapy (DBT) have improved thousands of lives, but not for every-one. Where I did find my peace and comfort was in books. I would spend hours lost in fictional novels of other worlds and excitements. I spent so much money that my husband announced one day that we needed to come up with a monthly allotment. (Thank goodness for Amazon Unlimited Books).

I would lie in bed after work, put in my earplugs, and read. There I was at peace. And at night, when my brain plagued me the most with thoughts of my brother's passing, I instead brought up imagines of my latest novel and created new worlds and themes in my head. Some people might read this and think I wasn't con-fronting my pain of losing my brother. However, that definitely was not the case. Reading helped me to be calm—to start remembering Jeff without breaking down. Books didn't stop me from thinking about him, but they allowed me a time of peace to give me strength.

Sometimes I also needed to cry and grieve, and I found that listening to music worked the best for me. My husband's aunt also lost a child about a year before my brother was killed, and she and I would exchange songs that helped us get out the tears. We found the songs from "Les Miserables" to be an excellent choice! If I don't find the time to cry when I desperately need it, my emotions become a ball lodged in my throat. For me, and for many, tears are cathartic.

Triggers sometimes set me back, and I need to find my comfort once again. I often give talks, and whether or not they are about my brother directly, they are always about mental illness and therefore include him indirectly. These talks can and do set me back emotion-ally. I tend to prepare by being alone and reading before and after a talk. I'm an introvert naturally, so it is even more important that I find time to be by myself. The point is to be prepared for triggers in the world and have outlets for when they occur.

Going to another person's funeral is also a trigger. I'm now much more aware of which services I can attend and which ones I need to support from afar.

Learning about a stranger's tragedy on the news or social media is another major trigger for me. I'm working earnestly on this one, because I can become highly emotional for another person I don't even know. These days I refuse to watch the news, because I know it just isn't healthy for me. In fact, I attended an event once where actor Joe Pantoliano (founder of *No Kidding, Me 2!*) spoke, and he said that the news was a major contributing factor toward his anxiety and depression. He even held up a doctor's note in which his psychiatrist had written on a prescription pad that Joe was not to watch the news. We cannot take away another persons' pain, nor does our suffering from the news make it any better for them. Going to that dark place doesn't help anyone.

I've become aware of most of my grief triggers, although some of them will pop up without my knowledge. It is important to have ways to go back to that comfort zone in order to reset. In fact, I have books on my phone, iPad, and Kindle, so I'm never without one.

I've heard that many people have success with some of the meditation apps out there. Yoga and walking have also been another source of comfort for me. Another tool is deep breathing exercises.

The most important thing to remember is to *not feel guilty* by finding your comfort zone. It's terrible being the survivor of sibling loss. But living happily and in a healthy way doesn't in any way mean that you don't love your sibling or that your grief has ended. Love is everlasting.

Chapter 13
You Are Not Alone:
Common Themes of Siblings

"I smile because you are my sister. I laugh because
there is nothing you can do about it!"

~Author Unknown

Six common themes keep cropping up as I interview siblings who
have a brother or sister with a mental illness. Many of these will
sound familiar, and remember—you are not alone.

Grief

Your world can fall apart for many different reasons: the loss of a
loved one; the loss of dreams; the loss of hope. Those who care about
mental illness issues often focus on what the parents are experiencing—and they should, because the mom and dad are going through
crisis themselves. It's very important, though, to not forget about
the siblings. They are grieving, too.

When I realized my brother's illness was not a quick fix, I started
to mourn the loss of my dreams for our future. He was my partner
in crime—the only one who would know me from childhood to
adulthood, the person who would help me take care of our aging
parents, and the one who would have my future nieces and nephews.

When a sibling is diagnosed with a mental illness, you feel lost
and unsure about how to help. The easy friendship is replaced with

stilted and unsure conversations. You grieve the loss of that special connection you had with your brother or sister from childhood. And, if your brother or sister passes away, you feel all of those losses again. This time, though, you also lose hope, and that is the greatest loss of all. Don't hide this grief from your parents. You must let others know what you need. Grief doesn't just disappear with time. It may evolve, and you will have to adjust your tools to help you through grief today.

Anger

It is natural to feel anger, but unfortunately, this is the one aspect of the situation that can break families apart. On my twenty-first birthday, my parents told me that I couldn't come home because of my brother's behavior. I was angry with him for separating me from my family. Another time, he kept talking on and on about God. I swear, I couldn't take the stuff coming from his mouth one more time. I was angry that he couldn't just snap out of it and realize that what he was saying was all gibberish. Sometimes you may be angry with your sibling, and other times you may be angry with the illness itself. At other times, I was just all-around irate. I mean, he was my brother. Shouldn't he have loved me enough to be well?

I interviewed one brother who told me that, because of his sibling's behavior, his family was blasted all over the media. This made him feel angry and humiliated. In a situation like this, you become the brother of the person who has done something questionable. Your own identity is removed and is replaced with your sibling's actions. The word "cooties" doesn't end in middle school—it lives with you for a lifetime. Whenever I tell people that my brother was diagnosed with a mental illness, they take a step back, as if it is contagious—or maybe *I* have it, and all of sudden I'm going to act out in a way that puts them in harm.

One sibling I know lost one of his parents because his brother took their mother's life. How can you still love someone who took away your mother? He is angry, but not always with his brother.

Most of the time he is angry with the illness, the lack of treatment options, and the stigma that prevented them as a family to seek help and guidance early on. He had to fight the system in order for his brother to be sentenced to a forensic hospital versus jail. This sibling literally had to defend the killer of his mom.

Although situations, like the ones I've described, cause siblings to be angry, the most common reason for their indignation is because their brother or sister who has the mental illness is slowly draining the lives and resources of their parents. And those parents do not listen to what the other siblings are trying to tell them.

Parents will tend to focus on the child who needs the attention, and often to the exclusion of the other children. While this is understandable to a degree, the other siblings must not be forgotten. I can't tell you the number of times I've had siblings fall apart in my arms because they've realized that they've held onto their anger and have lost twenty or more years with their brother or sister. They have lost family holidays and outings with their child's aunt or uncle, and now it may be too late. The anger is also understandable. All I can say is, allow yourself to feel the anger, but *don't let it define your relationship.* No one asks for mental illness. Try to redirect the anger and turn it into compassion.

Friendship Dynamics

It can get a bit interesting when, on a Friday night, your friends are going to happy hour, but *you* need to go to an inpatient psych hospital to visit your brother instead. It also can be difficult to relate to your friends when their "problems" seem almost silly compared to *your* stress and feelings of being in a constant state of fight or flight—unsure if your brother will survive another day and unsure if your parents can continue to handle the burden.

If your friends start to squirm when you talk about mental illness, then it's time to make new friends. One of my friends actually came with me to visit Jeff. It meant the world to me to not feel alone and have my friend with me to experience the loud clicking sound the exit doors make when they lock as you leave the person you love behind.

Communication

Siblings can make the common mistake of not talking to their brother or sister who has a mental illness. They are concerned about "rocking the boat." I get that. My brother used to go through times of self-harm. It is one of the scariest things to experience. He wouldn't eat and he was destroying his knees. We lived like we were walking on eggshells. When he was well and taking care of himself, the last thing I wanted to do was inadvertently say something that would take him back to that dark place.

While this is a real fear for siblings, your brother or sister with a mental illness probably is stronger then you give them credit for. My brother was the strongest, most courageous person I know. Anyone who has to deal with the stigma and discrimination that come with the label of "schizophrenia" is beyond amazing! One time my brother Jeff started rambling on about God, and I couldn't follow his thought process. I told him flat out that I didn't like what he was saying. He looked at me, saw the pain and fear that I was experiencing, and said, "Okay." From that point on, we started to talk more about his illness and his life. When I starting acting too much like a mother, he'd say to me, "Shannon, I need you to be my sister."

So, talk to your sibling. He or she is stronger than you think. Your brother or sister can tell you if it isn't a good time to talk right now. But don't assume. *Miscommunication leads right back to anger.*

Self-Care

At one point, I was working full time, my brother was in crisis and dealing with self-harm, and my dad had a heart attack. My body and brain were not in a good place. I couldn't sleep due to worry, I wasn't eating in a healthy manner, and I was feeling completely run down. Remember that in many crisis situations to take care of your needs first before helping others.

Take your B12 vitamins. Practice deep-breathing exercises (many guided apps are available). And let's be honest—while you may be able to look back and laugh at some moments, like having your brother strip naked and run around your neighborhood, there are traumatic moments that can happen, too. Talk to a therapist or a friend. And always remember that you are not alone.

Survivors' Guilt

This is the most hidden of all of the six themes. Why my brother or sister and not *me*? Will it happen to me? Sometimes I hear siblings say, "Why can't they just snap out of it?" Honestly, I believe some of those feelings are driven from a place of fear and guilt. We grew up in the same house, and we had the same parents. Why was I spared and not him? I still ask myself this question. I also questioned my faith. I don't have the answer, but I do know that none of this is your fault.

After my brother was killed, and after the funeral service, a friend of my father came up to him and asked him, "Well, aren't you relieved that you don't have to take care of 'him' anymore?" He didn't understand how thoughtless that question was. There is *nothing* about my brother that I would have changed unless *he* wanted it. He was not less of a brother for having an illness, and he taught me so much. His struggles made me a better person, and for that I will always be grateful. The only thing I *would* change is having him here to be an uncle to my two daughters.

Maintain some distance when you need it, but don't stay away. I can't stress enough the importance of communication!

To All Siblings Reading This Book

I know some of you are still holding onto anger. You may have become an expert at putting your feelings toward your brother or sister to the side, and convinced yourself that he or she has no real impact on your life. But your sibling *does* have an impact on your life. Yes, having a mental illness doesn't excuse his or her behavior or the pain you and your family are enduring. Therapists and friends will tell you to keep toxic people out of your life. And if you do that, I understand. However, do it with the full knowledge that such a separation *does affect you.* Some people decide to remove a person from their life and think that friends are replaceable. But a brother or sister is the only one you get. Maybe you and your sibling can't be together at this point in time. Maybe he or she has caused irreversible harm, but remember that doesn't mean the situation hasn't caused you trauma, post-traumatic stress, and grief. Even if you choose to cut ties with your sibling *you will still grieve the loss.* Life doesn't just become a bed of roses. And twenty years later when he dies, you will grieve again.

I'm not telling you what to do. Heck, I'm not even giving you advice on whether or not to keep your brother or sister in your life. What I *am* telling you is, whatever decision you make will impact you. I'm tired of hearing someone advise friends or relatives to cut someone from their life without talking through the decision, the impact, and, quite frankly, the future. Remember, too—if you have removed your brother or sister from your life, you have the right to bring him or her back into your life, regardless of what anyone (friend, therapist, etc.) says. The beauty of life is that nothing is permanent. That is reserved for death.

Let's talk about trauma for a minute. I don't list trauma as a seventh common experience because it is woven into all six of the other themes. We are traumatized, whether it's from the first time the police showed up at the house to take our brother or sister away, when we started to notice the anguish of our parents, or when we realized that our brother or sister might not make it to tomorrow. From my experience, many siblings have not dealt with the trauma they've lived through. There's a good reason for this. The sibling relationship is seen by society as not nearly as vital as other relationships in our lives. The message becomes: this trauma we have experienced is minor—just get over it.

And yet, if you pick up a book, both fiction and non-fiction, many of the dedications are to the author's siblings. Another perfect example of sibling love is the relationship between Prince William and Prince Harry, or Glenn Close and her sister. Being told as children that your brother or sister is a part of your inner circle, but then receiving the opposite opinion as an adult, just doesn't make sense. The trauma, pain, and anguish you experience from your sibling's mental illness are valid and real.

Chapter 14
Siblings' Actions: "Hot Button" Issues

"Calm is a Superpower."

~Author Unknown

Chapter 13, "You Are Not Alone: Common Themes of Siblings," was geared toward the emotions that siblings go through when their brother or sister has a mental illness. This chapter focuses on their *actions*. If you are not a sibling and are reading this chapter, please, do not judge. These are real struggles we go through. These are the most private thoughts that we experience due to the roller-coaster ride we go through when our brother or sister lives with a mental illness. Some of us have lost our siblings to suicide, others to jail, and others to drugs. Some of us have endured periods of time when a brother or sister has gone missing, only to be met with a friend's advice of, "let them go." Others of us have experienced stigma by association. In fact, a number of us have had our names shattered through the media because of actions by our siblings who have a mental illness. *All of us* have experienced trauma. Trauma creates anxiety, and with anxiety, we tend to over-analyze. Now let me explain the outcomes of this trauma and anxiety.

Hot Button Issue #1: Should I Have Kids?

I broke down in tears when the man who is now my husband asked me to marry him. I didn't know if he would want to have kids with me. Maybe I'm a carrier of a gene connected to schizophrenia.

Would he want to put himself through that when he could marry someone else without this kind of baggage? Or did he want to marry me and not have children so that we wouldn't even have to risk it? Did I want to have kids? I wasn't sure, especially after watching my brother, my parents, and myself suffer like we did. Schizophrenia is no joke. It's not something I would wish on my worst enemy. My brother was physically harming himself because of a delusion he was holding onto. I cried myself to sleep more times than I could count. So would I want to bring a child into the world in which that could possibly be his or her fate?

I can't answer this question for you. Just know that *it's okay* to ask yourself whether or not you want to have kids. After some serious thought, I realized that no matter what we were going through with my brother Jeff at that moment, I was so grateful for the nineteen healthy years I shared with him before his diagnosis. And even during the years after his diagnosis, we were closer than ever. This freed me from being scared about having my own children. Today, my husband and I have two wonderful girls. I admit that I find myself over-thinking their behaviors. Being educated about mental illness makes me constantly question if it is presenting itself. I've gotten better, but who knows what will happen when my children hit their teenage years. Yikes!

Hot Button Issue #2: Spouses

When my brother was in the hospital, I would visit him every other night. I never missed a visit. When he was in a locked, long-term-care facility, I also took him out on weekends. When he showed up at my house, I sometimes took him in. I took community college classes on mental illness. I quit my job and changed careers. I cried—a lot.

Our significant others care about us, and then they see us fall apart. We work ourselves to the bone taking care of the needs of our family and siblings. Eventually, these people we love are going to get frustrated. They may take this out on your sibling and/or your parents. They may try to prevent you from participating in your sibling's care or allowing him or her to visit anymore.

My best advice is to determine a plan on which you both can agree. If my husband felt like I was no longer taking care of myself (for example, not sleeping or eating properly), then I needed to take a step back from my brother's needs and focus on my own. By talking it out and agreeing on action steps, it eliminated frustration and miscommunication. This discussion may get heated, because a lot of love and emotions are involved. Consider seeking a third-party counselor, such as a marriage counselor, a spiritual leader, or a therapist, to help create your plan.

Hot Button Issue #3: Violence

Let's get real about this subject. Now remember, people with mental illness are no more violent than other people. In fact, most violence occurs by individuals who do *not* have a mental illness. Furthermore, the U.S. Surgeon General believes that only 4 percent of violent actions are caused by mental illness, and that people with mental illness are more likely to become *victims* of violence.

Even with these statistics showing that mental illness does not equate to violence, all of us have had wide exposure to media, social media, and the entertainment industry, all of which have skewed and twisted the truth of mental illness and violence. We've also heard the stories of a person with mental illness killing someone in a moment of delusion. Recent reports suggest that education reduces stigma about depression and anxiety but increases it regarding schizophrenia. Trying to combat these misconceptions is exhausting. Even with all of the knowledge you have, a part of you may be scared that your brother or sister will have a moment of violence. Even if it is just a tiny kernel in the back of your mind, it can drive a wedge between you and your sibling. In your spouse's mind, that kernel is much larger, because he or she wants to protect you. And if you have children, the kernel can turn into a wide chasm of fear.

Talk to your therapist, your spouse, and your support group. Monitor your "self-talk." The more you use terms like "deal with," "cope with," and "manage" in relation to your loved one, the more you focus on possible *behavior* rather than on the *individual*.

And you can't just make this feeling go away, especially if your brother or sister has exhibited moments of violence. Violence is not just physical harm—yelling or screaming can put you on edge as well. If you see signs of violence, you can tell your sibling's care provider. By law, you can share information with your sibling's mental health provider. Above all, your safety is paramount. Do not feel guilty for removing yourself from your sibling if you are feeling unsafe. Mental illness is not an excuse for violence or abuse. Don't let 'what ifs' or guilt plague you for making your safety a priority.

Hot Button Issue #4: Abuse

I feel fortunate that I never experienced this with my brother. Therefore, I can't speak to it personally. However, I want to acknowledge those of you who *have* experienced abuse, either physical or emotional, at the hands of your sibling. I recently read a blog from a mom who talked about the angst she experienced of being both the mother of the victim and the mother of the abuser. I've tried to not sugarcoat the sibling relationship in this book; however, I'm not an expert when it comes to abuse, and I can only hope for your healing journey.

Abuse is a form of trauma. Maybe you and your sibling can come to a place of reconciliation, or maybe you can't. Either way, do what is best for you, but know that what is best might not be what is easiest.

Hot Button Issue #5: Embarrassment

I can say with certainty that every sibling has experienced the emotion of embarrassment when it comes to the actions of his or her siblings. Maybe it is when your brother stripped naked running down a public road (which today I can laugh about), or maybe it's when you're sitting in a quiet movie theater and your sister bursts out laughing during a sad scene because of some internal dialogue that you are not privy to. Maybe your sibling did something that made the news and opened you up to everyone's ridicule. Embarrassment is a hard one. On the one hand, it is only natural to feel embarrassed when a person's behavior is outside of the box that our nation has deemed acceptable. On the other hand, after feeling embarrassed, you might also feel shame and guilt. Only other siblings can really understand the range of emotions you go through and how they can shift rapidly from one to another and back again.

My best advice is to find other siblings with whom you can talk, and know you are not alone. Try to not feel guilty for being embarrassed or for saying something you wish you could take back after a particularly embarrassing situation. I've been there, done that.

Hot Button Issue #6: The Truth About "Hitting Rock Bottom"

How many times have parents been told to let their children hit rock bottom—as if by doing this, the child they love, whose behaviors have changed due to mental illness, will "normalize" when he or she hits rock bottom? In fact, so the advice states, the bottom will force the child to climb to the top again. These statements have been repeated from one parent to another, from a provider to a grieving family member, and from the community to the family, over and over again. But because hitting rock bottom has never resulted in a cure for mental illness, why has this idea been perpetuated and carried on through the years? Hope. Hope is the reason why hitting rock bottom has survived as the fallacy it is. The belief that everything about the child you love can be fixed by simply allowing him or her to hit rock bottom is why this assumption has survived despite its perpetual failure of actually curing someone from a mental illness.

To be clear, the "hitting rock bottom" that I'm talking about refers to helping individuals who live with a mental illness (such as schizophrenia, anxiety, or bipolar disease) experience a full life in recovery from their illness. I'm not speaking of the use of "hitting rock bottom" in terms of recovery from addiction. I do see some parallels, however, as I believe that recovery takes a village, and maintenance takes love and support.

Let's analyze what "hitting rock bottom" means. Let's say your child has schizophrenia and suffers delusions of grandeur, flat affect, and hallucinations. You want your child to work, attend school, and find the love of his or her life. In this current state of illness, however, you know that cannot happen. And then you become upset and angry. In fact, you are grieving the loss of the dreams you held for your son or daughter. His or her behaviors are erratic—laughing at voices that are not there, being unable to hold a conversation, and getting fired from a job for the third time in six months. You've told your child to get on medicine, seek help, and participate in a support group—but you are talking to deaf ears. Another termination occurs, and this time your child has stripped naked and run down the street in front of your home. More anger, grief, and isolation set in. Now someone tells you, "You need to let your kid hit rock bottom." And if you allow that to happen, what's the result? Does your child suddenly see the light? Do the delusions or hallucinations disappear? Will your child magically decide that medicine is what will make a difference in his or her mental state? The answer is a resounding "no." But you've heard of this mythical bottom before, because it has been perpetuated over time. And when someone—friend or foe—says it to you, you have hope!

Let's apply this to your adolescent child who is dealing with depression and suicidal thoughts and has started to drink and smoke pot. Your teenager's grades have been dropping and you've received calls from the school about unexcused absences. His or her behavior at home makes you want to scream from the rooftops. YOU are in pain, you are scared, you don't know what to do or where to go, and you keep wondering how has this happened to your precious child. That morning, you argued with your child, and you demanded that he or she stop drinking and attend a group session. Then someone tells you to lock your teenager out of the house until he or she is clean and sober. Your child must hit rock bottom in order to recover. Hope flares. You say to yourself, "Yes—once my son (or daughter) has it hard enough, he (or she) will see the light and magically know how to get over this depression." I've never heard of persons recovering from depression and suicidal thoughts when they feel unloved by the very people who mean the most to them.

Today, even most addiction treatment professionals now eschew the "rock bottom" benefit. If a person is using alcohol and drugs to mask the symptoms of the illness, then isolation, separation, and loneliness are rarely the answers.

Hot Button #7: Hospital Visitation

"Your brother loves Skittles," the nurse told me with a smile. Warmth flooded her eyes. "I usually get him some toward the end of my shift. There's a vending machine down the hall." I smiled back at her and felt a sense of relief that someone at the hospital genuinely cared for my brother and not out of obligation to the job. It made it easier to leave him behind even when he gave me those puppy-dog eyes that he had been giving me his whole life to convince me to do something he wanted. It's funny—I actually see those same puppy-dog eyes when my youngest daughter wants something from her big sister, the ones that no one can resist and that are often followed by an eye roll, a sigh, and an "okay."

My brother spent many hours inside psychiatric hospitals. Everything about the hospitals made me question our decision to leave him there. It's not hard to see that the mental health care in a hospital is not the place that makes the business money. Unlike in the spinal surgery wing, mental health patients have low reimbursement rates and high personnel costs. This discrepancy is a very visual stigma. So when you get a nurse who does some simple gesture, like getting Skittles with her own money, it makes you want to cry. It makes you want to believe that people really do care.

Stigma is deadly.
Hope is healing.

What this nurse will never know is that she gave me—the sister—hope. That hope kept up my energy and my mind healthy, and it allowed me to come back day after day to visit Jeff. Visiting a loved one in a hospital isn't easy. It takes considerable energy, courage, and strength. Every night I went, I had to fight myself and all the excuses I'd make to not go. "He is fine; he won't miss me." "I will go tomorrow." "It's been a long day and I'm tired." "It isn't fair."

Visiting your sibling in the hospital is hard, but I recommend going. When I visited Jeff, I saw many other patients waiting in the chairs and looking at the doors with hopeful expressions on their faces that I was there for them. It broke my heart that their family and friends weren't there to visit. In fact, their faces kept me going back to see Jeff. I never wanted him to have that look on his face while he waited for me.

The first twenty-four hours are the hardest. Staff members usually give patients enough drugs when they walk through those doors that your loved ones appear to be shells of themselves. If you visit your sibling at that time, be prepared. Just sit with him or her. You don't even need to talk. Watch whatever is on the TV together. *Your presence is the most important piece.* If you go within seventy-two hours, the drugs probably will be more stabilized in your sibling's system. Bring cards and play gin rummy. Bring a coloring book and crayons, and just sit and draw or color together. Go for a walk outside. *Your presence is love, and love is healing.*

Hot Button Item #8: Jail/Prison

What do you do if your sibling is in jail? So many of us have some form of PTSD every time the phone rings, because too many times the call ends with bad news on the other end.

"Jeff is missing."

"Jeff was kicked out of the treatment program."

"Jeff lost his job."

"Jeff is back in the hospital."

"Jeff stole two bottles of wine and is jail."

Wine? Really? Don't ask. I doubt Jeff was ever a wine lover, but for some reason he decided to steal two bottles of it on a Friday night. My parents kept this from me and didn't tell me until Monday, when he was about to be released to their care. If you are a parent reading this, please know to *not keep secrets from your other children*. Finding out several days later is not protecting the siblings—it's only delaying the invariable discovery. It causes trust issues with the parents, feelings of guilt for having fun when the rest of the family was suffering, and irritation for not being included in the family. Just because siblings age, move out, and have families of their own doesn't mean they are no longer family. I think my mom was embarrassed by my brother's actions. Again—wine? Give me a break.

What do you do when your sibling has actually done something criminal? This is tricky, because a little voice in your head says that it doesn't want to deal with any of this crap. That voice makes you angry with your sibling. All of those excuses to not visit when your brother or sister was in the hospital come back tenfold, and this time you feel justified because his or her action was criminal. The government isn't forgiving your sibling's behavior, so why should you?

I have a friend who had a quote on her e-mail signature: "You might have fifty more years, or fifty minutes." You don't want any regrets. Check your anger. Seek a friend or therapist with whom you can talk. And then jump through the legal system in hopes of seeing your sibling. Now, obviously what my brother did was wrong, but it wasn't the end of the world. If you've been the victim of abuse by your sibling, then decide what is right for you and your family. Maybe you are in a place of forgiveness, and maybe you aren't. But if you are, remember that forgiveness only depends on you. Your sibling might not accept your forgiveness or even desire it, but it isn't your sibling's choice—it is yours and yours alone.

I love this quote from Eleanor Roosevelt, "Only you can make yourself feel inferior."

If you decide to visit, let me tell you here and now—it is a horrible experience. Visiting Jeff in a locked psych unit with a lady telling me how dangerous all "those" people were was nothing compared to visiting him in jail. No, he wasn't the drooling mess that I experienced in those first twenty-four hours of visitation at the hospital, but he still was a shell of himself. And this time, the shell was wrapped in fear. For the first time, I saw desperation like a cloak surrounding him.

My brother was diagnosed with schizophrenia, and, above all else, he had anxiety but never depression. He was the happiest person you could ever hope to meet. And because he loved people, he was destroyed when they abandoned him. I could take or leave people, but Jeff thrived on human connection. When I went to the jail to see him, my anger fled as my eyes saw him sitting there. He was truly alone, isolated, and scared. It didn't matter that he was twenty-two and I was twenty-six—I was transferred back in time and I was eleven and he was seven. I was holding his hand as we crossed the street and I walked him to school. He was four and I was eight, and I was putting a Band Aid on his knee after he fell. He was four days old, and I was four years old, and he was asleep in my arms.

If you choose to visit your brother or sister in jail, do it: (1) on your terms, (2) without anger, and (3) with a plan for *your* mental health after the visit.

Chapter 15
Being an Advocate for Your Sibling

"Help your brother's boat across, and
your own will reach the shore."

~Hindu Proverb

In order to talk about advocacy, you have to start with why being siblings is important. Did you know that there is a National Siblings Day? April 10 each year in the United States is the day to celebrate and honor the relationship of siblings. Yet how many people are even aware of this special day? What amazes me is that we are taught from infancy that our siblings are important. We must be gentle with them when cradling their blanket-swaddled bodies in our little arms. We must share our toys and attention. Social media lights up with pictures of children playing together and footage of an older sister/brother meeting the new addition to the family for the first time. In the United States, our culture values our *childhood* relationship with our siblings but treats it as secondary when we become adults. As adults, we are no longer encouraged to foster the relationship that was developed in our childhood homes. On the other hand, many authors dedicate books to their siblings, and innumerable story lines include sibling relationships. As a society, the adult sibling bond is seen as a secondary relationship, but clearly in our hearts it is important. Someone once told me that you only really know love when you have a child. As a mom of two, I love my children to the moon and back. But my four-year-old heart knew love the day Jeffrey was brought home.

Siblings share feelings for each other in a different way than any parent, spouse, or best friend ever can. By being born, your sibling defines you—you become someone's brother or sister. Now, instead of being an only child, your position in the family is suddenly changing. Whether you are a big brother or a little sister, your siblings play a critical role in who you are and who you will become. Sometimes the feelings you have for them are hard to define, but your siblings are the only other people who have gone through the same things and have grown up in the same way that you have. Whether your parents are still married or divorced, your siblings have been there with you to experience it all, through the good times and the bad. They have been with you for the major events of your childhood and have seen you cry and laugh, get in trouble and be praised, and fail and succeed. It puts all of you together in a unique situation, because you have an understanding that can't be shared with anyone else. I'm not saying that we can't create family out of friends, because we can and do. But even the best of friends usually aren't there when you wake up on Christmas morning and your little brother crawls into your bed bursting with excitement about opening his gifts from Santa. Nor are they with you when you hide behind a closed door and listen to an argument between your parents. You and your siblings share memories that no one else can possibly have. And, even if you and your siblings experience years of separation for whatever reason, you always understand that there are other individuals out there who "know" you.

When you discover that your sibling has been diagnosed with a mental illness, it is very frustrating, and sometimes loving your brother or sister is difficult. His or her behavior might be erratic and unpredictable, and once alcohol and drugs are added, you just want to throw your hands up in the air. All the warm fuzzies from your childhood become blurred with each phone call to the police or financial strain placed on the family.

You may be asking, what should I do? Should I start going to my sibling's doctor appointments? Should I pick up his or her medicine at the pharmacy? Should I write to my congressional representatives to demand changes?

And then your brother comes home with a busted lip because he drank so much that he jumped off the hood of someone's car and landed on the gravel below. The worst part is that he can't even remember what happened. Moments like this either encourage you to take action, or you retreat from the relationship you once had.

There are many ways to take on the role of "sibling advocate." If you live close to your brother or sister, you can be supportive of his or her everyday needs; however, be cautious that you advocate—not enable. You can advocate for the larger mental health community by creating and supporting programs that fill gaps or end stigma and discrimination. Or you can join your voice to thousands of others and demand changes in the insurance industry to promote mental health parity, access to treatment, and much more. In many ways, being a mental health advocate is a way of life, and with it comes a new and expanding family of supporters.

When it came to brother's mental illness, my natural instinct was to do something about it, and sometimes I wrapped myself up in my brother's problems to the point where he had to remind me that I wasn't his mother. What an eye-opening conversation that was, and it was pivotal in our relationship and in my role as a sibling advocate. That conversation allowed him to know how much anguish I was suffering because of his illness, and at the same time, it opened my eyes to the type of support, or *pestering*, that I thought I was giving.

I also learned how easy it is to assume you can "fix" the problem by taking care of your sibling. However, I also had to remind myself that the only person who can fix the situation is the *person with the illness*. Jeff was the one who had to cope and function with his illness, and I was just enabling him by doing the everyday, normal things a person should do. It is important as a sibling to be a strong support. In my brother's case, however, he needed to be able to care for himself, and if I was continually jumping in to help him, he'd never gain the skills he needed. As a result, I might eventually burn out and become resentful of all the work I was putting into his care, even if he wasn't asking for my interference.

It is hard to recognize when you have crossed the line from being a strong supporter to becoming an enabler. An example of enabling might be making all of your sibling's doctors' appointments or arranging your schedule to drive him there every time. It's important to realize that it may seem helpful, but what happens if you can't be there to do it? What if you have to care for your own children, or an important project at work needs your immediate attention? Through my work in the mental health community, I often see individuals who have a mental illness but don't know how to get their medication. In some cases, they don't even know what types of medication they are taking. This can happen when a parent, sibling, or spouse takes on the responsibility of getting the prescriptions, having them filled, and then doling out the medicine at the required intervals. *People with mental illness need to be directly involved in their own care beyond just showing up at the doctor's office.* You are being supportive if you remind your sibling to take the medication or if you ask if he or she took it. But it is your *sibling's responsibility* to actually decide to take the medication. Individuals with a mental illness need to know what they are taking, when and how much to take, what side effects might occur, and whom to contact if there is a problem with the medication.

Mental health medication has not been perfected and can lead to multiple physical health issues, including cardiovascular disease, type 2 diabetes, and premature death. Therefore it is critical your sibling understands the medicine he or she is taking in order to mitigate the potential side effects.

My brother and my work in the mental health community taught me that what we think is best for family members with mental illness isn't necessarily what they want or are capable of doing. For example, sometimes I would ask my brother, "Why don't you get a job?" or, "Why don't you go back to school?" My brother wouldn't do it, and I just couldn't figure out why. I mean, these were simple things, right? I was so frustrated because I thought that if he could get back into a "normal" life, it would help him recover. I now know that he couldn't at that time. He needed love and support, and sometimes a push in the right direction, but he also needed us to back off and work *with* him, not *against* him. Naturally, our hope was that my brother would be able to do these things, but the timeline we had created wasn't reasonable for my brother.

When you begin to realize that you are enabling your loved ones rather than supporting them, you may find it difficult to change your role—but it isn't impossible. Remember my story where my brother showed up at my door and needed a place to stay? It went against every cell in my body to tell him that he could not stay there, and it was one of the hardest things I've ever had to do. What made it possible for me to turn him away was remembering the old saying, "If you give a man a fish he eats today, but if you teach a man to fish he can feed himself forever." I knew I needed to teach my brother to "fish," even though my instinct was to take care of him. I found the phone number for a local shelter but had him make the phone call. I listened to him as he made the call, and I was proud of him. He was coherent, and he knew what he needed. I realized I had helped him gain a skill, even though it was hard for me to let him do that on his own. But I also was relieved, because I knew that if my brother was ever alone again, he'd know how to find a safe place to stay. That is the type of support a sibling can offer. You can stand by your loved ones and teach them how to take their medication or cook for themselves without doing it *for* them. Ultimately, your job is to love your siblings but let them struggle and thrive on their own. I know some of you are cringing and thinking well my sibling is much worse off than yours. That is the same excuse I've heard from hospital staff when we talk about working towards a zero restraint use policy. It is scary and I know you have a lot of fear from experiences in the past. And you don't want your brother or sister to ever end up back in the hospital, or in jail, or worse death. These are very real fears. But I have found to be true that when we treat someone as capable they will rise to the occasion. If we treat someone as inferior, they will believe they are.

The biggest lesson I learned from my brother's illness is to be an advocate *with* Jeff, not an advocate *for* him. Jeff was stronger and more responsible when he had the power to make his own decisions. It was my own lack of knowledge about mental illness that made me assume I knew better. In fact, if you ever watch the movie *Evan Almighty*, actor Morgan Freeman, who plays God, says, "If a person wishes for courage, does God give them courage or opportunities to be courageous? If a person wishes for their family to become closer, does God give the members of the family warm fuzzy feelings or opportunities to love each other?" I worked hard with my brother to encourage him and teach him the right tools so that he could have meaningful conversations with his doctor about his mental health care. Although I never abandoned my awareness of my brother's need for care, I did learn to step back and let Jeff do what was necessary—even if it wasn't what I would have chosen. It's a difficult process. Let's face it, life is hard. But because my parents and I learned to hold on loosely, Jeff became more capable and responsible for his own care.

Siblings also need to realize that they may become the direct caregivers and advocates out of necessity. If the parents pass away or encounter a situation that prohibits them from caring for the child with a mental illness, siblings may be the only persons who can step into the caregiver role. The ideal situation is when the parents and sibling(s) plan for this. My parents anticipated that I would become Jeff's direct caregiver and advocate as they became older. However, they wanted it to be as least intrusive as possible so that I could maintain my own life, and Jeff could maintain his. They set up a trust fund to cover his care and made arrangements for their home to be paid off so that Jeff could continue to live there once they passed away. It wasn't something any of us enjoyed thinking about, but I wanted to prepare myself for when I'd become responsible for my brother.

If you don't live together, there are other ways to take on the role of advocate. I clearly remember the moment when I decided to switch the course of my career and focus on changing the mental health field and the stigma that came with it.

Not long after the family visit to Jeff in Florida, where my brother was staying at a facility to help him with drug and alcohol problems, my parents received a call from a staff member telling them that Jeff was doing things beyond their capability to treat. The director said Jeff was kneeling—all of the time—and he wouldn't eat. He was again talking to himself very rapidly, switching from topic to topic.

My parents flew to Florida to bring Jeff home. When they returned, they took him to a doctor, and that is how and when Jeff was diagnosed with schizophrenia. When my brother was formally diagnosed with this mental illness, his friends left him one by one. "Schizophrenia" is a scary word. When people hear it, they think of the movie *Sybil* or of someone with multiple personalities, meaning, you don't really know who the "real" person is.

With the loss of his friends, Jeff became increasingly isolated. Even people whom he had known from the age of seven avoided him now. My brother craved interaction and liked being with people, and without anyone around, he started staying in his room for longer and longer periods of time. He was depressed, and although I regularly tried to get him to do things with me, even I couldn't get him to leave his room. Although he loved me, I was his sister, and what he really needed was a friend.

Just because I didn't know what else to do, I asked one of my friends who also knew Jeff to take him to the driving range. Jeff got so excited about going somewhere and having someone to do something with that he showered and shaved. His clothes were clean and even matched. That might seem like small things, but with Jeff and his illness, this was a big deal. He was coming out of his stupor and leaving his bedroom. Even his speech became more coherent. When this happened, I looked at my mom, and I knew what we were both thinking, "This is what he needs. More than medicine, more than cognitive therapy or any of the other stuff, he needs a friend." And that is what prompted me to become a mental health advocate for the larger community and start my nonprofit program.

At the time, I was in an MBA program, and I created a business plan for a nonprofit organization that would provide friendships to people faced with mental health challenges. My husband was very supportive of my interest and need to become an advocate, and I began pairing people from the community with those who had a mental illness.

When my nonprofit was starting, I had one problem—my brother knew about it. He was still struggling with the idea that he had a mental illness and even doubted that he really did. Knowing that I had created an organization to help those with a mental illness and was becoming more involved in the mental health community proved to my brother that I thought he had a mental illness. He thought that I somehow believed he was "less than" human. I had to walk a very fine line between getting Jeff to understand that he did have a mental illness without accusing him of having one. To society, "schizophrenia" is a bad word. In fact, research has shown that stigma has only improved in one category—people believe it is not a sign of personal weakness or that people do it to themselves. But if a person is asked if they are okay if their child marries someone with a mental illness, or if their coworker or neighbor has a mental illness, all of those values go down the tubes. I interpret this to mean that society believes mental illness is real and it is not anyone's fault, but you must maintain a 100-foot radius from such a person at all times. Sounds a lot like leprosy, and Jeff was more than aware of this.

Even though I knew Jeff was leery of my involvement with mental illness, and your sibling might be as well, I didn't stop. At first, when I began approaching community programs, the people there thought I was just some young girl who was going to come and go. They perceived me as a person who was ignorant enough to think I was going to single-handedly save the world, and when I discovered how hard it was, I would leave. Even though they weren't quite sure of me, they were also excited that a younger person wanted to do something. I discovered right away that people in these sorts of organizations were traditionally much older than me. When they finally began to trust me, and discovered that my dedication and interest were sincere, they signed me up for everything. This got me interested in another kind of advocacy, one that focused on policy changes.

As an advocate for policy change, I learned it is critical to listen to all sides, even ones you may not necessarily want to hear. Though you may have had a specific experience, it is important to know that your experience doesn't mean you know everything there is to know. Other ways or scenarios can, and should, impact the decision-making process. A psychiatrist on the news once said, "Well, if they (people with a mental illness) would just take their meds, then this (bad thing) wouldn't have happened." It is much too simplistic to say that a person recovers from just a pill. A poor advocate will focus on one way or one solution to the exclusion of all others. A poor advocate, for example, may have a family member who experienced great success with a certain medication and, as a result, advocates that other people with the same condition should be treated the same way. To inform people about your family member's success is valuable, but to assume it's the only way or even the right way for everyone else is not. To be a true advocate, you must understand that one treatment isn't the only way and that other people's input must be considered to create a fuller picture.

A good advocate is able to perform a balancing role. Anger does not equate to advocacy. When someone is diagnosed with a mental illness, it is all too common for the people around that person to become angry. They may be mad at the system or law or how they perceive treatment, but voicing that anger doesn't change people's minds. By going before a board of decision-makers, it doesn't help to vent frustrations and rant that a loved one's care isn't any good. Many people believe that if they "go down there and tell those people what to do," change will happen. But it just doesn't occur that way. You must voice your concerns but also balance those concerns with solutions and ideas for progress.

Policy change also happens by breaking down stigma and discrimination. Sharing your family's story and journey is one of those ways.

If you are interested in becoming an advocate, there are a many different ways to begin, and many various ways to be one. You can become an advocate for yourself or for someone who needs care. In my family, that was my parents' role. They became direct advocates for my brother, Jeff, and worked to ensure that he received appropriate healthcare and that his needs were met. Some advocates work on local, state, and national levels and focus on making changes through legislation. Siblings have the opportunity to be advocates on all three levels if they want to be.

The way I see most siblings becoming advocates is through the third type: acting as part of the community to change the laws. This usually happens because the parents are the direct caregivers, and therefore their time is constantly accounted for. However, siblings can make time to attend mental health board meetings, research laws, and participate in committees. Siblings assume an advisory role by learning what really can and cannot be done.

Often, after I talk about my brother and the work as I do as a mental health advocate, other siblings ask me how they can do more. But just so you know—not everyone can or should go the route I took. The one aspect about mental health is that everyone in every field can do *something*, because mental health affects the brain, meaning it literally impacts everything. If you are a reporter, do a positive story depicting mental illness. If you are an artist, give a class to people with mental illness on how to use art as an expression of their health, or go to The Giving Gallery to sell your artwork and donate a portion to a mental health organization. Create a walk team for the local NAMI. Tell your story.

Do I like what I do? It depends. Some days I fantasize about choosing a whole different career—of leaving everything related to mental health in the rearview mirror. Constantly scaling walls leaves something to be desired. Ultimately, though, by becoming active in the mental health community and being aware of what was going on in the mental health field, my parents and my brother Jeff became stronger and more comfortable with his diagnosis and care. Because Jeff was no longer a minor, he was ultimately in charge of his care, although my mom often accompanied him to appointments, and sometimes so did I. As I became an advocate, it helped my brother gain the strength to recognize that he was in charge of his treatment and could make positive decisions. When people visit the doctor, many get what is called "White Coat Syndrome." The patient has something wrong, and the doctor offers a prescription or some kind of treatment, but that isn't what the patient really wants. Instead of having an honest conversation, the person accepts what the doctor provides and leaves with the situation unresolved. With my support, I believe my brother realized it was okay to discuss with his doctor that his medications were bothering him or that he couldn't wake up in the morning and have a productive day because of them.

As a sibling, you are not powerless in this journey your family is taking. Being an active participant and educating yourself can make a difference to parents, the sick sibling, and even people throughout the community. Remaining quiet reinforces the stigma of mental illness, and running away stops the necessary care both you and your sibling need. People outside of the mental illness community need to hear what is happening so that changes can be made. Although it may seem that my advocacy was done just for my brother (and in the beginning that may have been true), it actually was a catalyst to bigger things. I couldn't be the parent, but I needed a way to make the situation better for my brother and my family, and becoming an advocate helped me do that.

They say you must be your own health advocate. Well, at this point in time, your sibling doesn't have a voice. Either help your sibling find his or her own voice, or use yours.

Chapter 16
How to Honor A Loved One Who Has Passed Away

"Grief must be witnessed to be healed."

~Elisabeth Kubler-Ross

"You are doing so much to honor your brother." These are words that were spoken to me by several individuals after Jeffrey was killed. I always managed a strained smile and a nod. No one wants to do anything "in honor of" or "in memory of" a loved one, because they would rather the person be alive and well. These words also make me feel guilty at times. Why did something so tragic have to happen in order for me to react? Every time someone says how proud my brother would be, or how he is he looking down on me from heaven with a smile because of the work that I'm doing to help those with a mental illness, a little piece of me feels tainted. It makes me question my worth as a human being—not to mention that I was working as a mental health advocate for six years before his death. Does this mean I wasn't doing enough? When I hear those words, I give my perfected smile and nod, then I work hard to get beyond what was just said. I try to keep plowing forward.

Maybe you feel the call to do something to honor your brother or sister but aren't sure what that looks like yet. For you, it has become important to find a way to keep his or her memory alive. Perhaps the world has stopped revolving for you, yet everyone around you is moving forward as if life is normal—as if the world didn't just lose an amazing person. It becomes important to you that the world *does* realize and remember that your sibling was here and that he or she was important and loved.

You might receive advice from different individuals on ways to honor your sibling. While you are working through what to do, it's a good idea to attend grief support groups. After Jeff was killed, we attended a program called GriefShare, a national organization that provides peer-based grief support for twelve weeks. For me, being surrounded by other people who had experienced loss was actually helpful. I was only twenty-nine when Jeff died, and none of my girlfriends had experienced any kind of major loss. They simply didn't know what to do or how to help. Two of my male friends had already lost their mother, so when Jeff died, the three of us had a special connection. I understood what it meant to enter a "new normal" or a "new" family. Over time, I've gathered many more people to become a part of my "new" life—individuals who have experienced similar losses and therefore know that grief has no timeline.

Support groups also exist for those who had a close relationship to the person who passed away but were not related, and for those who lost someone in a tragic manner. For example, if you lost your sibling to suicide, consider joining a local "survivor of suicide loss" support group. As you work on the trauma of losing your sibling, opportunities will arise on how to honor your brother or sister.

As you can see, I relive each memory of my brother as I write this book. I take the passion, pain, and angst and turn these feelings into honoring Jeff's memory. Telling my story about him is very important to me. It also tells the world about a guy you didn't get to meet but whose life still mattered and had meaning. And most important of all, he was loved.

Over the years, I've met people who find ways to raise money for a cause, such as creating a walk team to support a local National Alliance on Mental Illness (NAMI) group or an American Foundation for Suicide Prevention (AFSP) group. Others may create an event to raise money for what the individual loved, like animals, children, or the arts. Some people may start a non-profit around this passion/cause. When my cousin died in a car accident on Football Sunday, my uncle created a non-profit to teach teenagers about blue-collar jobs. He wanted them to know the many opportunities that are open to them—that if they decide college isn't the right fit, their worth is still great. Normally, I wouldn't recommend creating a new non-profit unless you've exhausted other options first. Non-profits are already spread very thin, and my wish is that more of them would give up their fiefdoms and merge together.

RI International, a non-profit organization, decided to honor my brother by creating the Jeffrey Christopher Award, which is given to an individual or organization that has made a major impact in the lives of individuals with a mental illness, particularly those who have been traumatized by the system and are working to change it. Every year at RI International's San Diego conference, they give out my brother's award with my parents in attendance. It keeps his memory alive and encourages mental health providers to go beyond the status quo—to break old traditions in favor of transforming the system.

As for me, I had been working with the local NAMI group and had put together a walking team to raise money. What else could be asked of me? I was angry by the way my brother died, strapped to a cold hospital bed in a small, gray, four-walled room, alone. That was my motivation to focus on patient rights. What did it mean for people with mental illness to have a "bad day?" How could we prevent more "bad days" inside hospitals? We need hospitals, but we need them to be helpful tools—not cruel places to be. Once trust is broken, it is very difficult to rebuild. After Jeff died, and with the help of other advocate groups like Disability Rights, I started to understand why others didn't want to go to a hospital even when they were in their worst state of mental health.

We were able to organize a group of nurses, doctors, hospitals, and other interested parties to evaluate the use of restraints. One of the problems we discovered is that we didn't really know how often restraints were being used and how long a patient was kept in them. The group helped to make public the data on restraint usage by hospitals. At the same time, NAMI California created an award to honor hospitals that had reduced and/or eliminated the use of restraints in their facilities. I wish I could say that there has never been another death by the use of restraints, but unfortunately I can't. Still, numerous efforts have been put forth to change and reduce this practice. I also created a website, www.recoverynotrestraints. org, so that individuals and providers could learn the myths and facts about the use of restraints.

Another way many individuals keep their loved one alive is by telling their story. You can create an Instagram account, a Facebook page, or a personal website. Share your story with The Mighty, the *Huffington Post*, or This Is My Brave. You may also e-mail your story to me (shannon@shannonjaccard.com), and I will post it on the Forgotten Survivors website. Telling your story lets others know that they are not alone. Even if we never meet, we share a close bond—a bond of healing and hope.

I'm in awe of Chester Bennington's wife, who has been sharing her husband's story. He died by suicide and she never let "shame" be a word in her vocabulary. She immediately shared a picture of him smiling and playing with his friends and family only four hours before he took his life. Her strength has been inspiring, and I'm sure it has had a bigger impact than she can ever know.

Let me remind you, though, that you *don't have to do anything*. Putting on a huge gala that raises a ton of money is wonderful. Carrying a picture of your brother or sister in your wallet or purse is also beautiful. Trust me, your loved one is not looking down at you from heaven and demanding that you one-up another sibling in order to prove your love and how much you miss them.

Love is love.

Chapter 17
The Impact of Mental Illness on the Whole Family

Whether you are a sibling reading this book, a parent, a friend, or a provider, everyone needs to understand how mental illness affects the whole family. I would argue that most illnesses, whether physical or mental, affect the entire family, but the medical community barely glances at the needs of the family. Caregiver support throughout the country is underfunded and overlooked. I continue to advocate that insurance companies be allowed to spend money on coaching and counseling for caregivers of individuals with a mental illness. Caregivers are an underutilized asset in the treatment aspects of mental illness.

Families are woefully unprepared for taking care of a loved one with a mental illness, and by most accounts, they generally feel like the illness showed up overnight. With the current lack of education and dialogue surrounding mental illness, it is no wonder that most families don't know what to do when faced with this difficult situation.

In 2016, AARP named those who take care of someone with a mental illness as the most invisible caregivers. Nearly half (48 percent) of caregivers said it was difficult to talk with others about their loved one's mental or emotional health issues (as reported in *On Pins & Needles: Caregivers of Adults with Mental Illness,* a study conducted by the National Caregiver Association, Mental Health America, and the National Alliance on Mental Illness). The study also stated that many parents go into a self-induced isolation over their child's mental illness. They tend to keep their struggles hidden from friends, from their church, and even from other family members. Those who care for family members with a mental illness reported providing this care for twice as long as for any other chronic health condition, and 74 percent reported that this caregiving is stressful. One third of participants reported their physical health to be only fair or poor. These statistics really shouldn't surprise anyone, yet caregivers are forgotten, dismissed, and oftentimes displaced from their social networks.

Every time my brother went missing, my heart rate increased from the anxiety I felt. I couldn't eat or sleep until he was found safe. Each time his mental health deteriorated, my fight-or-flight response would overreact, and I suffered because of it. Every time my brother was rejected, his emotional pain would be my own.

Everyone's health in the family circle suffered. My dad had a heart attack, my mom's dormant Lyme's disease became active, and I developed abdominal problems. Almost every family member I know who is a caregiver or loss survivor has some sort of physical health condition. These range from multiple sclerosis to stress related physical issues like eye twitching, itching fingers, and premature signs of aging. I have wondered why insurance companies do not spend more money on caregiver support. If we had the tools we needed to care for someone with a mental illness, then our bodies would stand a better chance of staying healthy. This, in turn, would reduce the need for costly medical intervention.

It is well known that stress kills. Being in a twenty-four-hour state of engaging your parasympathetic nervous system is stressful to the body because you are constantly releasing damaging hormones—not to mention how you probably aren't able to make time to do healthy things for yourself in order to combat the negative appearance of stress, like eating right, exercising, drinking the necessary amount of water. Or even doing simple things that calm your mind, such as reading a book, watching a movie, or getting sleep.

The fact that our bodies are falling apart does not stop us from caring for the person we love with a mental health condition. For caregivers, there is no down time in which to heal.

When my dad had a heart attack, my brother was residing in a new board-and-care facility. I use the word "care" loosely, because this was another place that "healed" by controlling the patients and demeaning their opinions. My mom picked up my brother, and we were all at the hospital when my dad was in surgery for a stint procedure. My brother was physically there—but psychologically he wasn't present. I don't know if it was the stress of seeing my dad in a hospital bed, or all of the lights flickering, or the machines making noise, but it was as if my brother had stepped away from his physical body. My mom was torn between who needed her more—Jeff, or my dad.

On top of everything, my dad wasn't concentrating on healing when his son was clearly unwell. I have to say, that was the day I hated mental illness. I hated my brother. My faith abandoned me that day. If my dad had died in the hospital, I don't know if I could have forgiven my brother. You might be shocked by my words, or you may remember a time when you felt the same way. In that moment, mental illness had stripped us of everything—a healthy brother, a healthy family, a normal outlook for the future. I wanted to take Jeff by the shoulders and shake him until he snapped out of it. Logically, I knew that none of this was his fault, but all I could see was my father dying, my mom not being able to focus on my dad, my dad not being able to focus on himself, and Jeff having all the attention to himself and not even trying to be *normal*.

Today, I'm still trying to fix some of the health-related damage to my body. After my dad's heart attack, when my brother wasn't doing well (not eating, always talking about God, and laughing for no reason at all), I went through a period of insomnia. Believe me when I say that not being able to sleep is at the top of my list for most horrible things I have ever experienced. To lie in bed, hour after hour, becoming more anxious with each minute that passes, knowing you have to get up soon without sleep, is emotionally and physically painful.

I've always been a night owl, and sleep never came to me easily, but I never felt like I *couldn't* fall asleep until I stayed the night at my parents' home. My dad was healing from the heart attack, and my parents needed some respite and support. They had already changed their work schedules so that someone was with Jeff twenty-four hours a day. My mom was a schoolteacher and worked during the day, and my dad drove a truck for FedEx in the evening. My brother would easily stay up until 2 a.m. He was staying in the bedroom upstairs, and I was in the room directly below. Every time I tried to close my eyes to sleep, I would hear him pacing. He sounded like a caged cat, just walking back and forth. Hearing this constant movement upstairs prevented my body from relaxing enough to fall asleep. Eventually, at some point in the early morning hours, I finally crashed when my body couldn't stay awake any longer—only to have to wake up a few short hours later to dress and go to work. I was so exhausted at work that I thought this couldn't happen two nights in a row, but boy, was I wrong. Much later, I continued to have problems falling asleep and decided to seek professional help.

You may be wondering if the physical and emotional toll of loving someone with a mental illness is all worth it. You may feel exhausted from living in a constant state of fear and uncertainty of what today will bring.

When my brother was killed, a friend of my father said to him, "Well, you've suffered with him for long enough." Many people I've shared this with have gasped after hearing this, but some will wonder if he was right. I was once at a support group meeting with a mother who was in crisis. *We often say that the person with a mental illness is in crisis, but in truth, the whole family is thrown into crisis at these moments.* In her grief, this mother made a comment that her son's schizophrenia was causing him so much suffering that maybe he would be at peace if he were no longer with us. If you have had these same thoughts, you are not alone. When you live 24/7 for another person, never knowing if today he or she will eat, sleep, or do drugs, it becomes a never-ending cycle of exhaustion with no end in sight. But let me tell you that, as a sister who is now an only child, death is much worse. When your loved one is still alive, no matter where he or she is at this very moment, there is still hope. Hope is real. Recovery is real. Don't let anyone tell you differently. And many people will try.

Unfortunately, words of discouragement may come from providers, family members, friends, and even folks within your own support groups. My parents once went to a support group for other parents who have a child with a mental illness. An older member told my mom that Jeff wouldn't get any better—that he would be on drugs for the rest of his life and they should just get used to the way he is. In essence, he was saying there was no hope that my brother could live a fulfilling and rich life. My parents never went back. I have been fortunate to see firsthand that *recovery is real,* because I became a mental health advocate. I was surrounded by people who had a mental illness and were living well with it. In fact, 75 percent of my staff had a mental illness when I was CEO of NAMI San Diego. Today I know national speakers, authors, and providers who are living well and thriving with their mental illness.

If, as I've described above, caregivers have a role in their loved one's life, then why is our input dismissed? Mental health providers see our brothers and sisters for very short moments in time, while we see them all the time at their best and their worst. More than 70 percent of those surveyed in the *On Pins and Needles* study stated that their loved one with a mental illness either lived at home or within twenty miles. So why isn't our input valued? In fact, I've often heard from siblings that they felt their input wasn't valued even within their own home.

I attended a day conference for family members who had someone with a mental illness, and the coordinator had arranged everyone in circular tables with eight people at each table. We were asked to answer three questions as a group and present our responses. One of the questions was: "John has a mental illness and lives with his parents. He feels that he is ready to move out but isn't sure how to go about having this conversation with his parents. His sister Suzy agrees with him and offers to help talk to their parents. What can Suzy do?" The question was geared toward what the *sister* could do in this family dynamic, yet not one person in the room answered the question that way. Everyone invariably answered what the *parents* could do to ensure their son's success. Unfortunately, this result wasn't surprising to me. To the parents reading this book, siblings have an inside track. We know our brothers and sisters in a different and unique way. Providers should not dismiss input from the parents, nor should parents dismiss input from their other children.

Families are the number-one caregivers for people with a mental illness. If they are not given the support they need, then how can the person with the illness possibly recover? The situation turns into a revolving door. The police are called, the loved one is taken for a short stint at a psychiatric hospital, the loved one is released to his or her home, the family has a short respite, the loved one gets home, anxiety and worry increase as the loved one starts exhibiting symptoms again, family health and communication deteriorate, then the police are called. Does this sound familiar?

Let's be honest—what family member or caregiver can practice self-care when:

- About one in three report that their loved one has been arrested (32 percent).

- One in five caregivers report that their loved one has been homeless for a month or longer (21 percent).

- Two-thirds of mental health caregivers are concerned that their loved one will self-harm (68 percent) or die by suicide (65 percent).

When I consider the thought of self-care for caregivers I recall what flight attendants say to you right before takeoff. They tell you to put on your *own* oxygen mask before assisting another person. That same rule applies to you as a caregiver. Be sure to start by taking care of yourself. Follow my tips on sleep. You may also want to practice yoga and do breathing exercises. You may like meditation or other self-guided visualization practices. Although it is very difficult to make the time for self-care, and although it is way too easy to ignore, if you love your family member who has a mental illness, you must first take care of *yourself*.

One of my favorite quotes is, "Time you enjoy wasting is not wasted time." Feel free to lounge on your couch and watch a movie if that's what you need to maintain your health! Discover what works the best for you, then give yourself permission to do it.

Epilogue
How I'm Doing Today

I've read several other books and memoirs on grief, and many had a last chapter on how they were doing today. For me, it's kind of an interesting question. As of this moment in time, I'm doing well, but how well I will be doing tomorrow is a mystery.

I will never stop missing my brother and no one should ask me too. And I will never stop being a sister even though my brother is gone.

During the process of writing this book I was overwhelmed by the number of siblings that I spoke with that had a story to tell, and in the same breath overwhelmed by how many doors kept closing in front of me.

Siblings are the best kept secret. Eighty percent of Americans have one, and yet we rarely discuss how our siblings impact our lives. And how we impact theirs. While we go on to have our own immediate families, our brothers and sisters were a part of our first families.

My goal for this book is that if you are a sibling of someone with a mental illness - know that you are not alone. You have experienced love, trauma, empathy, and fear. And you deserve to have your voice heard.

Please speak up.

I believe that working and talking with siblings is the missing ingredient to improving our mental health system. Our combined voice can demand better quality and access to care, it can help remove barriers such as stigma and discrimination, and create new policies that positively impact mental health care.

You are important and your story matters.

You are not forgotten. You are a survivor.

Let's share our stories.

Shannon

Endnotes

PART I

Chapter 6

Substance Abuse and Mental Health Service Administration (SAMHSA) www.samhsa.org

PART II

Chapter 11

Carlos
Lopez, Linette. "THE SIBLING EFFECT: 12 Amazing Facts About Brothers And Sisters." *Business Insider Online.* Sept. 2011. Quote by Jeffrey Kluger, author of The Sibling Effect, in an interview with Salon Media Group.

Sisters
Goleman, Daniel. "Men at 65: New Findings on Well-Being." *The New York Times.* Web. Jan 1990.

Pharoh
Dutta, Sharangee. "Here Are 16 Interesting Facts That Science Has To Say About Siblings." *Scoop Whoop.* Web. Feb. 2016.

Danielle
Kluger, Jeffrey. "The New Science of Siblings." *Time Magazine.* Web. July 2006.

http://content.time.com/time/magazine/article/0,9171,1209949-2,00.html

Sam

Dutta, Sharangee. "Here Are 16 Interesting Facts That Science Has To Say About Siblings." *Scoop Whoop*. Web. Feb. 2016.

Trudy

"15 Fascinating Scientific Facts About Siblings." *Nursing Schools. net*. Web. May 2011.

PART III

Chapter 16

Grief Share is a friendly, caring group of people who will walk alongside you through one of life's most difficult experiences. You don't have to go through the grieving process alone.

Contact: https://www.griefshare.org

Chapter 17

On Pins & Needles: Caregivers of Adults with Mental Illness, a study conducted by the National Caregiver Association, Mental Health America, and the National Alliance on Mental Illness. To review report, go to: https://www.caregiving.org/wp-content/uploads/2016/02/NAC_Mental_Illness_Study_2016_FINAL_WEB.pdf

Resources

SIBLING SUPPORT

Sibling Support
Contact: https://www.siblingsupport.org
Description: Founded in 1990, the Sibling Support Project is the first national program dedicated to the life-long and ever-changing concerns of millions of brothers and sisters of people with special health, developmental, and mental health concerns.

Sibling Australia
Contact: http://siblingsaustralia.org.au
Description: Promoting better support for siblings of children and adults with disability

Rethink Mental Illness
Contact: https://www.rethink.org > carers & family > brothers and sisters
Description: Welcome to Rethink Mental Illness. We help millions of people affected by mental illness by challenging attitudes, changing lives.

GENERAL SUPPORT

Depression and Bipolar Support Alliance
Contact: www.dbsa.org
Description: Depression and bipolar disorder can be isolating illnesses, but DBSA support groups can help you connect with others

who have been there as well. Visit a DBSA support group and get the support that is essential to recovery.

National Alliance on Mental Illness (NAMI)
Contact: www.NAMI.org
Description: NAMI, the National Alliance on Mental Illness, is the nation's largest grassroots mental health organization dedicated to building better lives for the millions of Americans affected by mental illness.

Mental Health America (MHA)
Contact: www.mentalhealthamerica.net
Description: Mental Health America (MHA) – founded in 1909 – is the nation's leading community-based nonprofit dedicated to addressing the needs of those living with mental illness and to promoting the overall mental health of all Americans.

Crisis

Crisis Textline
Contact: text HOME to 741741. https://www.crisistextline.org
Description: Text from anywhere in the USA to text with a trained Crisis Counselor.

Every texter is connected with a Crisis Counselor, a real-life human being trained to bring texters from a hot moment to a cool calm through active listening and collaborative problem solving. All of Crisis Text Line's Crisis Counselors are volunteers, donating their time to helping people in crisis.

National Suicide Prevention Hotline
Contact: (800) 273-TALK (8255)
Description: A free 24-hour hotline available if you or someone you know is in suicidal crisis or emotional distress. Press 1 for a dedicated line for veterans and their families.

About the Author

Shannon Jaccard is a behavioral health consultant and adjunct professor in the field of health care services Alliant University. She was the CEO of the National Alliance on Mental Illness (NAMI) San Diego and Founder of Compeer San Diego. Shannon serves on several boards including RI International, The Meeting Place Clubhouse, and San Diego County Behavioral Health Board. Shannon has received numerous awards such as; the Rona and Ken Purdy Award to End Discrimination and the Channel 10 News Leadership Award. She was named one of San Diego's "50 People to Watch" by San Diego Magazine. Shannon has published several articles bringing to light the experiences siblings share when a loved one has a mental illness and is an international speaker on stigma, labels, and mental illness. Shannon has a blog for siblings on grief, loss, and shared experiences. Shannon earned her bachelor's degree in political science from the University of California, San Diego (UCSD) and her Master's of Business Administration from California State University, San Marcos. Shannon is an Aspen Institute Fellow of the inaugural class of the Health Innovators Program and a member of the Aspen Global Leadership Network.

Contact Shannon:

Shannon@shannonjaccard.com
www.shannonjaccard.com

You can also follow her on social media:
Instagram: www.instagram.com/shannonjaccard
Facebook: www.facebook.com/shannonjaccard
LinkedIn: www.linkedin.com/in/shannon-jaccard-m-b-a-b48ab110/
Twitter: www.twitter.com/shannonjaccard